Praise for

Little Women, Big God

"In her new Bible study, Debbie brings new perspective on how to see ourselves in the lives of these unlikely women. Some were abused and broken, some crushed under the weight of despair, and even one young unqualified girl was chosen for a big purpose. These pages filled with truth helped me to realize the wonder and matchless love that a Big God has for this little woman. May all my days be spent boldly living out that love and truth."

—**Amy Richissin,** development officer, Turning Point

"Women in the Church today are hungry for excellent Bible study material, and this book will be a blessing to those who use it. I have spent my retirement years teaching a women's Bible study at my church. Guess which book will be the focus of the next study? It will be such an encouragement for women to relearn the lesson that God has tried to impress upon our hearts since the birth, life, and resurrection of our Savior: we all have a role in God's divine plan, and we should never underestimate what our mighty God can do with lives that are surrendered to him."

—**Diane Passno,** Bible teacher (retired), senior vice president,
Focus on the Family

"Are your problems threatening to crush you? Debbie Wilson's outstanding book, *Little Women, Big God,* shows you where to take them. *Our help comes from our big God.* Take a deep breath, settle down, pull yourself together. Help and hope are here."

—**Nancy Cobb,** national and international speaker, author of multiple books,
including *The Best Thing I Ever Did for My Marriage*

"Today's challenges are not new to God. Using the stories of the women of old, *Little Women, Big God* shows you how to overcome your trials."

—**DiAnn Mills,** author of *Deadlock* and *Deadly Encounter*

"We all have a story to tell, a story worth telling, a story that is an intricate part of God's great story of hope. But deep down we wonder if God can really use us. In these ten in-depth studies of women in the Bible, Debbie Wilson opens the door to how God worked in their lives . . . and how he works in yours. The insights you gain will enable you to face your struggles, look deeply into the eyes of the gracious Jesus, find hope and healing, and discover the empowering and equipping you need to tell your story."

—**Rich Miller,** president, Freedom in Christ Ministries-USA; author; speaker

"Debbie Wilson makes each woman in this study so real and timely—the challenges each women faced ARE relevant to us today. Debbie skillfully opens our eyes to this connection. *Little Women, Big God* is refreshing, thought-provoking, and encouraging while showing us that nothing is too big for God. This is one Bible study you don't want to miss! I truly didn't want it to end."

—**Lisa Grimes,** president and CEO, PurThread Technologies, chair, Lighthouse Ministries

"With the timeless power of God's Word, Debbie Wilson fearlessly addresses issues that crush modern women and make them feel small. From familiar problems like fertility to forgiveness, Debbie gently leads us to follow the examples of women in Scripture who have wrestled and found God's healing solutions."

—**Amy Carroll,** Proverbs 31 Ministries speaker and writer, author of *Breaking Up with Perfect*

"Debbie Wilson has the gift of bringing God's Word to light and doesn't disappoint in her latest book, *Little Women, Big God.* Her wisdom and insight are sure to enrich the spiritual life of any reader. I highly recommend *Little Women, Big God.*"

—**Diane Rumley,** co-founder, Support Military Spouses

"What an incredible study on this precious tapestry of little women with a BIG GOD! Each week you will have the joy of looking at life from a different woman's example of truly experiencing God in the midst of life's joys and challenges. Thank you, Debbie, for drawing us to our BIG GOD, who loves each of his little women with such an intimate eye on our lives. May each of you who choose to go on this journey learn that our God is a creative Father, who has a very personal plan and purpose for each of his daughters!"

—**Nancy M. Wilson,** Global Ambassador/Cru, author, speaker, StoryWave director

"I love Debbie Wilson's Bible studies. She always brings a fresh perspective from Scripture and shows me another view of Truth. When I read her material I am always empowered to make wiser, stronger choices and I am freer to be who God created me to be. She is a perfect blend of Grace and Truth, and *Little Women, Big God* is no exception."

—**Jane S. Wolfe,** founder and executive director, Dew4Him Ministries, Inc.

Little Women BIG GOD

I dedicate this book to three little women who've made a big impact in my life. To Virginia B. Woeltjen, my late mother, who showed me unconditional love. To Diane W. Deans, my sister in blood, spirit, and faith, who has shared and enriched life's journey. To Ginny Wilson, my daughter, friend, and cheerleader, who splashes every occasion with joy and fun.

And to the women who do this study, may each of you enjoy the love and grace of our Big God.

Little Women BIG GOD

IT'S NOT THE SIZE OF YOUR PROBLEMS, BUT THE SIZE OF YOUR GOD.

Debbie W. Wilson

LEAFWOOD
PUBLISHERS
an imprint of Abilene Christian University Press

LITTLE WOMEN, BIG GOD
It's not the size of your problems, but the size of your God.

an imprint of Abilene Christian University Press

Copyright © 2016 by Debbie W. Wilson

ISBN 9780-89112-386-6

Printed in the United States of America

Published in association with The Blythe Daniel Agency, Inc., PO Box 64197, Colorado Springs, CO 80962.

Cover design by ThinkPen Design, LLC | Interior text design by Sandy Armstrong

Leafwood Publishers is an imprint of Abilene Christian University Press
ACU Box 29138
Abilene, Texas 79699

1-877-816-4455
www.leafwoodpublishers.com

Table of Contents

Acknowledgments 8

Introduction: *Jesus' Surprising Family Tree* 9

May I Introduce You . . .
Personality Test 15

Week One: Tamar—
When You Need Grace 19

Week Two: Rahab—
When You Long for Unshakable Faith 45

Week Three: Ruth (Part 1)—
When You Grieve 77

Week Four: Ruth (Part 2)—
When You Are Empty 103

Week Five: Bathsheba (Part 1)—
When You Are Desperate for a Bath 135

Week Six: Bathsheba (Part 2)—
When You Yearn for Supernatural Strength 159

Week Seven: Bathsheba (Part 3)—
When You Hope to Move Forward 183

Week Eight: Mary the Mother of Jesus (Part 1)—
When You Face the Impossible 213

Week Nine: Mary the Mother of Jesus (Part 2)—
When You Dream of Peace 235

Week Ten: Your Story—
When You Gotta Tell Somebody 257

Notes 269

Acknowledgments

First of all, I want to thank my wonderful husband, Larry, for loving me unconditionally and giving me a tangible example of our Savior's love. You encouraged me to develop my spiritual gifts, even at the expense of domestic chores!

I must also thank my daughter, Ginny Wilson. She used the study with her friends and offered feedback and encouragement. You are my special cheerleader. To my son, Brant Wilson, you continually enrich my life with your depth, artistic eye, and by making me pause and observe the beauty of life's gifts.

A special thanks goes to Lisa Grimes and Sandi Brown for their encouragement and practical support. Where would I be without you?

I am also indebted to the women who went through the study with me, offered their feedback, and encouraged me along the way. And, of course, the prayers of my friends and small groups fueled the process.

A big thank you to my agent, Blythe Daniel, and the Leafwood Publishing team. In a multitude of counselors there is victory! (Prov. 24:6 paraphrase)

Most of all, my deepest gratitude goes to our Lord Jesus, the big God who continuously carries this little woman.

Introduction
Jesus' Surprising Family Tree

Do you find yourself praying for an undemanding life? I do. Green lights, good health, cooperative clerks, computers that work—bring it on. I choose easy.

Yet movies and books without obstacles or danger don't hold our attention. And aren't simple games or effortless contests usually *boring*? Challenges not only add spice to entertainment, but they help us grow.

Sometimes when life is hard, I take it personally. Is God disappointed in me? Has he forgotten me? Maybe that is why the women in Jesus' genealogy speak to me. They lived hard lives. Some faced humanly impossible circumstances. Yet they grew closer to God in their trials and experienced his incredible strength and comfort.

Their stories made me realize I'd been praying the wrong prayer. Instead of asking God to make my life easy, I should be asking for his grace to be strong. What a difference that small switch made in my attitude! Jesus' words—"Take heart! I have overcome the world" (John 16:33)—were spoken for trials, not for days of ease.

Do you fall apart when life gets tough? Does stress make you act ugly? I have. But our failures don't nullify God's grace. The women in our study show us how to experience his presence, power, and peace in our weaknesses.

Real Women—Just Like Us

"Wow, you sound like Abraham," I said to a man who'd told me about the adventure of a new career. He flinched and assured me he'd never presume to be in the same category as a biblical personality.

I wonder if that's how you feel. Have you ever put Bible characters on a level so far above that you can't relate to them? If so, I think you'll be surprised and delighted to meet the women in Jesus' family tree. They are like us.

This isn't an elite group of celebrities who enjoyed the pampered lives of the rich and the famous. Some were poor and destitute; only one lived in a palace. Neither are they a bunch of supersaints. Some made bad choices and doubted God's good intentions. Some of the women in Jesus' genealogy are familiar, such as Jesus' mother, Mary. Others, such as Tamar, are less known. As you read their stories, identify with them as real women.

- How would you have felt?
- How would you have responded?

From their stories, you'll learn the value a big God brings to an ordinary life. You'll also see how God has chosen you for a significant role in his eternal story.

Open Your Heart—Not Just Your Book

This ten-week study is divided into nine weeks of looking at the women in Jesus' genealogy and one week of fashioning your own story of faith. Each week is divided into five daily lessons. Questions will stimulate your thinking about the passage and its application to your own life. Allow them to guide you, and feel free to ask your own questions. Take the thoughts I offer that work for you and discard those that don't. My desire is to help you to be a thinker and an able listener to our great God. He desires a close relationship with you!

Some questions are personal. If you are studying this with a group, contribute only what you are comfortable sharing. But remember, we enrich one another when we open up with each other. Day five includes a wrap-up of the week's thoughts.

I Want to Remember . . .

At the end of each day's lesson, write down any statements that will help you recall what God is teaching you. Don't feel pressured to be clever. You are capturing the insights the Holy Spirit revealed to you. They can be bits of Scripture, thoughts you underlined, or personal applications. I think it would be fun if we encouraged each other by sharing them on Twitter with the following hashtag: #LittleWomenBigGod

Tips

We're all busy, but we make time for what we value. I make time to brush my teeth, bathe, and eat. Why? Because I know the personal and social benefits of these habits.

God created us and knows what our day will hold before it begins. If Jesus needed to meet with his heavenly Father each day, I need to also. Many call this meeting a quiet time or personal devotions. When we show up for our quiet time, we have God's full attention. He will speak to us through his Word, the Bible. What could be more valuable than hearing from God each day?

Plan for your time alone with God by answering these three questions.

When? Pencil in on your calendar the times in the upcoming weeks when you will meet with him. Guard that time as strictly as you would a doctor's appointment. Keep your rendezvous with God. A woman shared with me, "It's amazing—when I schedule my quiet time, I have the time. I feel so much more peaceful."

Do you want the strength that comes from unshakable faith? "Faith comes from hearing the message, and the message is heard through the word about Christ" (Rom. 10:17). I need God's perspective each day. Between visits, my problems seemingly grow. When I renew my mind, I remember how big God is. Problems shrink to proper proportion.

If you haven't begun this daily discipline, make this small commitment and schedule your time. The benefits are eternal.

Where? Select a special place to have your quiet time with God. When you keep your tools—Bible, workbook, pen, and whatever else you use—where you study, you associate that place with meeting the Lord, and your heart begins to look forward to this treat.

How? Start by inviting the Creator of the Universe to speak to you today. Exercise your faith muscles and thank him for meeting with you. Open your heart and believe God wants to speak to you from his Word.

Some people read Scripture with a harsh tone in their minds. Jesus calls himself gentle and humble. He does not speak unkindly to his children. His warnings and corrections are spoken in love to protect us. Satan misused Scripture when he tempted Jesus. He twisted God's warning when he spoke to Eve. Learn to separate God's voice from the critical voices that may play in your thoughts.

God won't be angry with you if you miss your special appointment with him. These are just suggestions to help you live strong. He enjoys meeting with his children, and we need time alone with him. Plan for success.

The Bible provides timeless principles for life. As you will see in the lives of the women we will study, these principles work even in challenging situations. If quality of life is determined by the size of our challenges, the women in Jesus' genealogy would have missed out. They had little strength, clout, or worldly resources to face their giants, but they had a great God. They prove the size of our God—not the size of our problems—brings fulfillment. How big is your God? Open your heart to him today.

May I Introduce You...

To introduce the women we'll be studying in the following weeks, I thought it would be fun to find the woman that best matches your personality. Beside each trait, put the number that best describes you.

- 1 — never
- 2 — sometimes
- 3 — often
- 4 — always

Tally your score under each character. The one with the highest score is your soul mate. Have fun!

Personality Test

Tamar

I take calculated risks. _____

I expect you to keep your promises. _____

I love children. _____

I'm patient to a limit. _____

I'm a careful planner. _____

I have clear goals. _____

I can read others. _____

Total _____

Rahab

I'm daring and bold. _____

I'm decisive. _____

I'm a natural leader. _____

I'm a negotiator. _____

I'm resourceful. _____

I take care of my family. _____

I'm unconventional. _____

Total _____

Ruth

I respect authority, but I stand up for my convictions. _____

I'm loyal to those who've been good to me. _____

I'm closer to my family of faith than my family of origin. _____

I'm compassionate. _____

I'm not afraid of hard work. _____

People say I'm quiet but courageous. _____

I remain steady through the highs and lows of life. _____

Total _____

Naomi

I'm outspoken. _____

I see things as black or white. _____

My emotions color my thinking. _____

I'm expressive. _____

I'm persuasive. _____

I break rules that don't make sense. _____

I'm a nurturer. _____

Total _____

Bathsheba

I forgive easily. _____

I'm compliant. _____

I ignore gossip. _____

I use life's experiences to instruct others. _____

I may not speak up for myself, but I will for others. _____

I give second chances. _____

People say I'm poised. _____

Total _____

Mary

I'm reflective. _____

I'm a worshipper. _____

I'm flexible. _____

I believe God for the impossible. _____

I'm not easily shaken. _____

I'm peaceful. _____

I'm steady. _____

Total _____

Are you ready to meet these women? Good! Let's jump into Tamar's story and see what we can learn from her walk with God.

When You Need Grace

Tamar means "palm tree."

Tamar's small hands trembled when she placed the veil upon her head. The men of this family had used her to get what they wanted. Her jaw tightened. No more waiting for a so-called follower of Yahweh to keep his word. This time she would take what she wanted.

TAMAR'S STORY SOUNDS MORE LIKE A TABLOID FROM TODAY'S headlines than a Bible story. Her drama usually isn't found in children's Sunday school lessons.

The Bible doesn't gloss over its characters' sins. Jesus' own lineage shows humankind's need for a Savior. In many ways, Tamar represents us. She couldn't save herself. As we'll see, God had to step in to rescue her from wicked husbands and redeem her from her own wrong choices. Tamar will show us God's grace in action.

Family Background

Before we look at Tamar, let's set the stage. God called Abraham to leave his family and go to the land that he would show him. He promised to bless Abraham and multiply his descendants, and he chose Abraham's family to represent him to the world. In fact, God promised to bless the whole world through Abraham's seed.

Jesus is the promised Seed that would bless the world. He is the Lion of Judah, the long-awaited descendant of Abraham's great-grandson Judah.

Abraham and Isaac lived among the Canaanites and were well aware of their shameful habits. They begged their sons not to not marry Canaanite women (Gen. 24:3, 37; 28:1). God later banned intermarriage to protect Israel from joining their sinful practices. But Judah married a Canaanite named Bathshua and chose another Canaanite, Tamar, to be the wife of his firstborn son (Gen. 38:2, 6).

What expectations do you think a young bride from this background might have marrying into a family of spiritual blue-bloods? Tamar, no doubt, shared the hopes and dreams of any bride. She stepped from her culture of serving pagan gods into a family that was supposed to serve Yahweh, the one true God. But Tamar's husbands did not live up to their high calling. This family, set apart to bless the world, caused her much pain.

An evil husband is a liability in any culture. But Tamar lived in a society where women were virtually powerless. With no property or reputable means to support themselves, women were dependent on their male family members for shelter and food.

Day One
Wedding Bells and Death Knells

Every bride wants to be cherished and secure. What happens when she feels trapped and used? Have you ever felt powerless, alone, unimportant, invisible, or used by those in positions of power? Does God care when we are abused or stuck? Does he rescue only the blameless?

Tamar will show us that no life is so obscure, so insignificant, or so dark that God's grace can't reach in and rescue it. Draw hope from God's care for Tamar.

Scripture Reading...

GENESIS 38

Study and Reflection

1. We know God cut Er's life short because of his wickedness, but Tamar may not have known why he died so young (Gen. 38:6–7). His wickedness is not explained. Remembering a time you felt abused may help you identify with what Tamar felt.

   a. What do you think it was like for Tamar to be married to an evil man?

   b. Do you think Tamar knew why he died? What kind of emotions do you think Tamar felt after he died?

2. How would you feel if someone who shared your name (in family or business) carried a disreputable reputation? Has this happened to you?

3. Also referred to throughout the book of Ruth and in Matthew 22:24, the law of the levirate (from the Latin meaning "husband's brother") was widely practiced and later became part of the Mosaic Law. This custom sounds distasteful to our modern ears, but it served a practical purpose. From Deuteronomy 25:5–10, explain why a childless widow was given to her deceased husband's brother.

4. What made Onan's actions so wicked to God (Gen. 38:8–10)?

5. Some religious groups have used Genesis 38:8–10 to support the view that God is opposed to birth control. Do you think *this passage* teaches that God is against birth control and that is why God killed Onan? Why or why not?

6. Judah and his two sons wronged Tamar. The custom of keeping the widow in the family prevented the extinction of the family member's name and provided the widow a means of support. Instead of fulfilling his duty and giving Tamar a child, Onan used Tamar for sexual pleasure and robbed her of an heir. Put yourself in Tamar's bed.

   a. In her culture, could Tamar save herself from these terrible marriages? How?

   b. How might this affect her?

7. How did God rescue her from these marriages, and what does that tell you about God's involvement in the secret sorrows of our lives?

8. What hope does this offer you when you feel trapped or used?

——

When have you lacked the resources to free yourself from a bad marriage, loneliness, debt, illness, addiction, anger, fear, gluttony, or a bad mood? In such times, did you long for grace? Being helpless is a perfect way to experience the Almighty.

I Want to Remember . . .

Write down any statements from today's lesson that will help you recall what God is teaching you. Let's encourage each other by sharing them on Twitter with the following hashtag: #LittleWomenBigGod

Today's takeaways from #LittleWomenBigGod are:

Day Two
Scandal

"Two wrongs don't make a right." Mama's words remind me that we feel justified in wrong actions if we think we're evening up the score. The abused becomes the abuser. Hurt people hurt people. Tamar followed this pattern and turned from victim to avenger. Have you ever created a mess you couldn't fix? In times like that, we need grace.

Scripture Reading...
GENESIS 38:8–26

Study and Reflection

1. Judah told Tamar to "live as a widow" in her father's house after Onan's death (Gen. 38:11).

    a. How did Judah view Tamar after his sons' deaths?

    b. How was sending her away treating her like an outcast?

    c. What challenges might Tamar experience returning to live under her father's roof?

2. Judah saw Tamar as the common denominator in his sons' deaths.

    a. When have you been unjustly blamed for something because the accuser wanted to protect himself or herself or the real culprit?

    b. Have you faulted others to protect yourself or someone else from just allegations?

3. A "long time" has passed since Onan's death. The son Judah had promised Tamar is grown. Judah has ended his time of mourning for his wife who had died after Onan. Yet Tamar still wears widow's garments (Gen. 38:12, 14, 19). Desperate people do desperate things. When Tamar realized Judah didn't intend to have her marry his youngest son, she disguised herself as a prostitute and sat at the gate through which Judah had to pass. How do Tamar's actions show insight into her father-in-law's character (Gen. 38:12–23)?

4. How did Judah react when he heard his daughter-in-law was pregnant (Gen. 38:24)?

5. What does Christ call those who practice double standards in the following verses? "For in the same way you judge others, you will be judged, and with the measure you use, it will be measured to you. . . . You hypocrite, first take the plank out of your own eye, and then you will see clearly to remove the speck from your brother's eye" (Matt. 7:2, 5).

6. What did Judah do when he recognized his signet ring, cord, and staff?

Two Wrongs: A Case for Grace

Tamar and Judah were both wrong to use illicit sex to meet their needs. Judah added hypocrisy to his sexual sin.

Our society still practices double standards. For example, pornographic venues are called adult entertainment, as if reaching a certain age makes it okay to violate God's moral standards. We too exhibit hypocrisy. Have you ever yelled at your child, "Don't raise your voice at me"? God graciously helps us with our blind spots.

After Judah's guilt and hypocrisy were unmasked before the world, he confessed, "She is more righteous than I." Being exposed was the grace he needed to repent. His change becomes evident later in Genesis when he pleads to become a slave in place of his brother Benjamin (Gen. 44:33). Admitting failure is the first step to healing change. Ask God to reveal your double standards and free you from your blind spots.

I Want to Remember . . .

Today's takeaways from #LittleWomenBigGod are:

Day Three

Sex—Special or Spoiled

A young woman phoned me, confused. Her longtime boyfriend was pressuring her to have sex. "He says he'll leave me if I don't. Is it wrong to have sex with him? We plan to marry one day."

What should the caller do? Does her choice matter? How do we know what's right? Are right and wrong determined by our culture or family's values? Thankfully, God has recorded timeless principles to guide and protect us.

Sexual immorality, in the New Testament, comes from the Greek word *porneia*. It is defined as adultery, fornication (sexual intercourse between people who are not married to each other), homosexuality, lesbianism, intercourse with animals, and sexual intercourse with close relatives.[1] The Greek word *porneuō* is also translated as sexual immorality in the New Testament. It means to prostitute one's body.[2]

Avoiding sexual temptation begins before an encounter. It starts with moral convictions that affect our motivations, dress, and conversations. First Timothy 2:9 tells women to "dress modestly, with decency and propriety." Tamar wore a veil. That sounds modest. But she was dressed in temple prostitute attire. Temple prostitutes wore veils to create the illusion that the sexual act was taking place with the goddess being worshipped. Just as red lights have been used to signify areas of prostitution, Tamar's veil identified her as a temple prostitute.

To avoid sending the wrong message, Christ's followers must dress not only with appropriate modesty but also with suitable awareness of our culture's interpretation of symbols. Let's see why God values sexual purity.

Study and Scripture Readings

1. Our culture glamorizes illicit sex and calls moral standards outdated. What does God say and why?

   a. Flee from sexual immorality. All other sins a person commits are outside the body, but whoever sins sexually sins against their own body. (1 Cor. 6:18)

   b. But among you there must not be even a hint of sexual immorality, or of any kind of impurity, or of greed, because these are improper for God's holy people. . . . For of this you can be sure: No immoral, impure or greedy person—such a person is an idolater—has any inheritance in the kingdom of Christ and of God. Let no one deceive you with empty words, for because of such things God's wrath comes on those who are disobedient. Therefore do not be partners with them. For you were once darkness, but now you are light in the Lord. Live as children of light. (Eph. 5:3, 5–8)

c. It is God's will that you should be sanctified: that you should avoid sexual immorality; that each of you should learn to control your own body in a way that is holy and honorable, not in passionate lust like the pagans, who do not know God; and that in this matter no one should wrong or take advantage of a brother or sister. The Lord will punish all those who commit such sins, as we told you and warned you before. For God did not call us to be impure, but to live a holy life. Therefore, anyone who rejects this instruction does not reject a human being but God, the very God who gives you his Holy Spirit. (1 Thess. 4:3–8)

2. Based on God's principles, how would you answer the young woman in today's opening?

Safe Sex

"Why is God ruining my whole life? I mess up one time, and I have to pay for it the rest of my life?"

How many times do we blame God when the consequences of our bad choices catch up with us? We jump over the guardrails God has put in place to protect us and then accuse him of ruining our lives when we suffer the inevitable crash.

Marriage is a guardrail for sex, and sex is God's sacred gift to marriage. God wants married couples to enjoy one another sexually (1 Cor. 7:5). Sexual intimacy depicts the holy union Jesus has with his bride, the church. Perhaps that is why it has been attacked and misused so much by the world.

The woman in today's opening paragraph refused to have sex with her boyfriend, and he broke up with her. She joined a Bible study and realized she wanted to marry a different kind of man— a man who would cherish her instead of use her to satisfy his own lusts.

If she'd given in to her boyfriend's demands, she might have married him. But she knows she would have regretted it. Years later, when she married her husband, she thanked God that he had saved her for a godly man who loves and esteems her.

Onan's selfishness turned the marriage bed into a place of misery for Tamar. But sorrow isn't the only indicator that sex is being abused. Consider couples where both enjoy the sex they share outside of marriage. Even if no one feels hurt during the relationship, from God's viewpoint, a lot is wrong. Our enemy knows its destructiveness, too. "Poland's Communist government even encouraged young people to have premarital sex, specifically to cause them to break from the church."[3]

Sex serves as mysterious glue between partners. Consider what happens when you separate two sheets of paper that have been glued together. One or both will rip. God's guideposts on keeping sex within marriage protect our hearts from being torn apart or becoming callused. They shield us from senseless heartbreak and regret.

God's Word is a *grace note* to those who receive it. His grace notes warn us of travel hazards on the road of life much like my Waze phone app alerts me to problems that affect my driving route.

God's wisdom shields us from regret, from unnecessary harm, and from having to perform to be accepted. His grace notes teach healthy self-respect and protect the joy of sex in marriage. Let God's grace notes guard you from false intimacy, imitation love, and counterfeit security.

Study and Reflection

3. Do you think Tamar wanted to have sex with her father-in-law? What motives could have been at work in Tamar to cause her to do this?

4. Tamar seized an opportunity to grab what she wanted. Her motives are not clear. Was she seeking a child, vengeance, justice, or security? Whatever her goal, she did not seek God or practice his wisdom. In what ways have you been tempted to meet your needs outside of God's will?

5. Women today willingly endure many ordeals in the hope of conceiving a child. From the following, how do we know which ones are acceptable to God and which ones are not? "Do not conform to the pattern of this world, but be transformed by the renewing of your mind. Then you will be able to test and approve what God's will is—his good, pleasing and perfect will" (Rom. 12:2).

Whose Wisdom?

I'm sure Tamar loathed the idea of being with Judah. Her husband had treated her like a prostitute. She must have decided she could endure one more humiliating encounter.

Desperation causes us to do things that go against who God wants us to be. Unlike an aggressive street prostitute, Tamar let Judah approach her. She used his weakness for her own purpose.

God had already liberated Tamar twice. Did she know God instigated her rescues? I wonder how many times he's intervened on your behalf and mine and we've not realized it.

Tamar took things into her own hands. If Judah wouldn't give her Shelah, she'd get a child, security, or payback another way. It's not wrong to want children or justice. Trouble comes when, instead of bringing our longings to God, we rely on our own understanding. God's wisdom agrees with his Word. His ways don't violate his moral standards.

Fertility clinics have helped many, but some of their advice opens a Pandora's box of trouble and reminds me of the problems Sarah and Abraham faced when they tried the culturally accepted—but not God-directed—practice of using Sarah's maid, Hagar, to fulfill their longing for a child.

When friends or professionals speak, especially when they promise what we want, we may be too quick to jump on their advice. I wonder if the person who told Tamar that Judah was coming helped plan her scheme. When a dentist said if I'd replace my filling with a crown, I'd never have to touch my tooth again, I was thrilled. Now I know crowns aren't permanent and bring other issues. In other words, even with nonmoral issues, don't be afraid to ask questions or take the time to seek God. The wisdom of the day, regarding morals or solutions to our longings, can't compare with the wisdom of the ages.

I Want to Remember . . .

Today's takeaways from #LittleWomenBigGod are:

Day Four

Tamar, a Look in the Mirror

How did you react to Tamar's story? Did you feel compassion for her? Or were you disgusted with her? What about Judah?

Some stories make me scratch my head and wonder why God recorded them. At first glance, this is such a story. Yet, isn't Tamar's story so much like ours?

Maybe you don't identify with Tamar. Let me draw some parallels.

Scripture Reading

ROMANS 5:8
But God demonstrates his own love for us in this: While we were still sinners, Christ died for us.

ROMANS 6:14
For sin shall no longer be your master, because you are not under the law, but under grace.

ROMANS 7:1–6
[1]Do you not know, brothers and sisters—for I am speaking to those who know the law—that the law has authority over someone only as long as that person lives? [2]For example, by law a married woman is bound to her husband as long as he is alive, but if her husband dies, she is released from the law that binds her to him. [3]So then, if she has sexual relations with another man while her husband is still alive, she is called an adulteress. But if her

husband dies, she is released from that law and is not an adulteress if she marries another man.

⁴So, my brothers and sisters, you also died to the law through
the body of Christ, that you might belong to another, to him who
was raised from the dead, in order that we might bear fruit for
God. ⁵For when we were in the realm of the flesh, the sinful passions aroused by the law were at work in us, so that we bore fruit
for death. ⁶But now, by dying to what once bound us, we have
been released from the law so that we serve in the new way of
the Spirit, and not in the old way of the written code.

Study and Reflection

1. God showed mercy to Tamar *before* she knew him. How did
    he show mercy to us before we knew him (Rom. 5:8)?

2. Tamar could not save herself from her terrible marriages.
    From Romans 7:1–3, why did God have to take the lives of
    her wicked husbands to free her (Gen. 38:7, 10)?

3. We were born wedded to our sinful nature. What is the only
    route to freedom from bondage to sin and the condemnation
    of the law (Rom. 7:4–6)?

4. According to Romans 7:4 and the following verse, who died?
    "I have been crucified with Christ and I no longer live, but
    Christ lives in me. The life I now live in the body, I live by

faith in the Son of God, who loved me and gave himself for me" (Gal. 2:20).

5. According to Romans 7:5, what happens to the person bound to sin?

6. Judah viewed Tamar as the problem. He tossed her out of his household and told her to remain a widow (Gen. 38:11). How is her experience a picture of us before we knew Christ? See the following verses. "Therefore, remember that formerly you who are Gentiles by birth and called 'uncircumcised' by those who call themselves 'the circumcision' (which is done in the body by human hands)—remember that at that time you were separate from Christ, excluded from citizenship in Israel and foreigners to the covenants of the promise, without hope and without God in the world" (Eph. 2:11–12).

7. Judah wanted to burn Tamar alive when he learned she was pregnant. When he recognized his cord, staff, and signet ring, he confessed, "She is more righteous than I, since I wouldn't give her to my son Shelah." God exposed Judah's intentions and other sin against Tamar. He had not given her to Shelah. It is easy to point out someone else's mess and ignore our own. What do you learn from the following?

   a. "You, therefore, have no excuse, you who pass judgment on someone else, for at whatever point you judge another, you are condemning yourself, because you who pass judgment do the same things" (Rom. 2:1).

b. "For the word of God is alive and active. Sharper than any double-edged sword, it penetrates even to dividing soul and spirit, joints and marrow; it judges the thoughts and attitudes of the heart. Nothing in all creation is hidden from God's sight. Everything is uncovered and laid bare before the eyes of him to whom we must give account" (Heb. 4:12–13).

8. Judah's transformation began with awareness of his need for cleansing. Why is it healthy to welcome the Holy Spirit's correction in our lives?

9. Now that we have been identified with Christ's death, we are no longer bound to sin or under the law. How does that change how we live and what we produce (Rom. 7:4, 6 and the following verse)? "For sin shall no longer be your master, because you are not under the law, but under grace" (Rom. 6:14).

10. By dying to sin and the law, we are now free to be joined to our new husband (Rom. 7:4). The church is called the bride of Christ. From the following, what does that mean for you?

c. "For your Maker is your husband—the LORD Almighty is his name—the Holy One of Israel is your Redeemer; he is called the God of all the earth" (Isa. 54:5).

    d. "Husbands, love your wives, just as Christ loved the
church and gave himself up for her" (Eph. 5:25).

What Am I Reflecting?

Do you struggle more with receiving grace or with giving it? If
we see ourselves as self-made, earn-your-way type of people, we
may not appreciate grace. But we should. The Pharisees in Jesus'
day didn't value grace. But those who recognize their helpless
state without Christ embrace it.

Tamar couldn't save herself from two bad marriages. Under
the law, the only way out was death. God intervened and rescued her.

You and I were like Tamar. We were married to evil men who
used us for their own lusts. Our husbands were our old natures.
We were their slaves. Because we were one flesh, we couldn't
get away from them. They owned us. This union brought pain,
shame, and disgrace. Under the law, only death could set us free.

To dissolve our union with sin, Jesus died in our place. Our
faith in Christ identifies us with his death, burial, and resurrection. God now sees us as crucified with Christ. We have been
raised with him and given a brand-new identity that is no longer
bound to sin. We no longer live under the law. We now live
under grace (Rom. 6:14). We have been set free to flourish in our
new union with Christ (Rom. 7:1–6).

Tamar no longer had to climb into bed with Onan and be used
like a sex slave. His death freed her. We no longer have to participate with sin's degrading passions. Christ's death has freed us.

Tamar lived as an outcast, separated from life with Judah's
family. We were hopeless outcasts, excluded from life in God.
But Christ made us family.

Judah and Tamar had their sin exposed. This caused Judah to acknowledge his unrighteousness. When the motives of our hearts are revealed under the light of God's Word, we are able to freely confess, "I've fallen short of God's glory."

God granted Tamar twins. Perez, the older, grew into a fine man whose name became a blessing (Ruth 4:12). God made Tamar a blessing to the world. God's grace creates a 180-degree change for us, too:

- Death to life.
- Barrenness to fruitfulness.
- Bondage to freedom.
- Despair to joy.

When we base our acceptance on our performance, we pressure others to meet our standards. We condemn ourselves or blame others when we fail. When we accept the grace God has provided, we joyfully pass it on to others. Grace allows us to give up working for the acceptance we already have in Christ.

Is there a Tamar in your life who needs your grace? Maybe it's you.

I Want to Remember . . .

Today's takeaways from #LittleWomenBigGod are:

Day Five
Redemptive Grace

Onan used Tamar for sex. Tamar used sex to entrap her father-in-law. If God chose people based on how good they are, God would not have picked Tamar or Judah for their astonishing roles in his story.

Tamar's ignoble actions did not squash God's grace. Scripture remembers her as the mother of the great man Perez and an ancestor of Jesus. Perhaps King David named his daughter Tamar after her.

Isaiah 62:4 reminds me of God's grace to Tamar—and to us. "No longer will they call you Deserted. . . . But you will be called Hephzibah [my delight] . . . for the LORD will take delight in you." No matter how badly we've blown it, God's grace is greater still.

Scripture Reading..

RUTH 4:12
Through the offspring the LORD gives you by this young woman, may your family be like that of Perez, whom Tamar bore to Judah.

RUTH 4:18–22
This, then, is the family line of Perez: Perez was the father of Hezron, Hezron the father of Ram, Ram the father of Amminadab, Amminadab the father of Nahshon, Nahshon the father of Salmon, Salmon the father of Boaz, Boaz the father of Obed, Obed the father of Jesse, and Jesse the father of David.

MATTHEW 1:1–3
This is the genealogy of Jesus the Messiah the son of David, the son of Abraham: Abraham was the father of Isaac, Isaac the father of Jacob, Jacob the father of Judah and his brothers, Judah the father of Perez and Zerah, whose mother was Tamar, Perez the father of Hezron, Hezron the father of Ram.

Application and Reflection

1. Tamar played the role of a prostitute with Judah. When have you blamed your wrong behavior on your extenuating

circumstances? What do you learn from the following? "For it is from within, out of a person's heart, that evil thoughts come—sexual immorality, theft, murder, adultery, greed, malice, deceit, lewdness, envy, slander, arrogance and folly. All these evils come from inside and defile a person" (Mark 7:21–23).

2. According to the following, how did God show grace to Tamar and to us?

> But because of his great love for us, God, who is rich in mercy, made us alive with Christ even when we were dead in transgressions—it is by grace you have been saved. And God raised us up with Christ and seated us with him in the heavenly realms in Christ Jesus, in order that in the coming ages he might show the incomparable riches of his grace, expressed in his kindness to us in Christ Jesus. For it is by grace you have been saved, through faith—and this is not from yourselves, it is the gift of God—not by works, so that no one can boast. (Eph. 2:4–9)

3. We aren't told if Judah was involved in the raising of his twins. Considering how Tamar and her son Perez are remembered in the book of Ruth 4:18–22 (today's reading), what might this reveal about this single mother?

4. In what ways can you identify with Tamar?

5. Recall a time when God showed you favor when you clearly didn't deserve it.

6. Tamar is the first woman Matthew mentioned in Jesus' family tree. Sarah, Rebekah, and Leah, also in Jesus' lineage, aren't even named. Now that you've studied Tamar, why do you think the Holy Spirit included her?

7. What thoughts do you have from Tamar's story?

When You Need Grace . . . Lessons from Tamar

Have you ever wondered how God could choose scoundrels like Judah to have significant roles in his story? The New Testament explains: "He has saved us and called us to a holy life—not because of anything we have done but because of his own purpose and grace. This grace was given us in Christ Jesus before the beginning of time" (2 Tim. 1:9).

Grace is shocking. Sometimes it even seems unfair.

When we understand God's holiness and our sin, we'll no longer approach God on the basis of our own merit. Who can go through a day, let alone a life, without a wrong thought or careless word (Matt. 5:21–22, 12:36; James 2:10)? Understanding our need for grace makes us revel in Judah and Tamar's story.

Mercy may be described as *not* getting the punishment we deserve. Grace is receiving a pony when we deserve a time-out. God's ultimate grace came when Jesus took the hell I deserved and gave me his heaven.

Grace is a stumbling block to the self-righteous. It doesn't seem right to offer heaven to sinners. But God looks at our hearts, where we've all fallen short of his glory.

God's grace affects more than our afterlife; it encompasses all of life. Ironically, it takes grace to recognize we need God in the first place. We all need his favor in a variety of ways. Tamar needed grace to endure her lonely marriages and grace to redeem her moral failing. Perhaps God used these needs to create a thirst for him.

Apparently, Tamar came from a family that did not know the God of Abraham. Judah was Abraham's great-grandson, yet he and his sons seemed to have no more compassion than the godless men of her pagan society. How would a woman from such circumstances ever come to know the one true God?

We aren't told how she came to faith, but in 1 Samuel 2:30, the Lord says: "Those who honor me I will honor, but those who despise me will be disdained." The fact that Scripture repeatedly names Tamar in genealogy lists and holds up her son Perez as an example to follow leads me to believe her life was transformed. Perhaps this happened when the Hebrews moved into Egypt under Joseph's protection.

Grace for the Trapped

God saw Tamar's private pain, apparently before she even knew him. Twice he rescued her from wicked husbands. Did she recognize his intervention? Had she prayed for help?

What agony do you suffer in secret? Do you believe our Lord sees and cares? Have you invited him into your suffering?

Grace for Unfulfilled Longings

The drive to escape pain makes us more vulnerable to options we would shun in better times. After her husband Er's early death,

Onan's wickedness, and Judah's superstitions blocked her hope, Tamar schemed to get what she wanted—what was rightfully hers.

"Hope deferred makes the heart sick" (Prov. 13:12). Have you ever felt heartsick over unfulfilled desires? Tamar longed to throw off her widow's garments. Her arms ached to cradle a child. Besides raising her status in society and offering financial security in old age, a child promised Tamar the companionship her marriages lacked.

Insisting on our desires may exclude God's best for us. If he seems to be ignoring your request, trust his wisdom and love. Waiting is sometimes necessary to prepare us for his best. Remember: "No good thing does he withhold from those who walk uprightly" (Ps. 84:11b ESV).

Anything we want more than God is an idol. Fully surrender your idols to him.

Tamar was wrong to play a prostitute, even for one day. Gaining the desired result did not justify her method. God granted grace to Tamar in spite of her sin. He gave her not only a baby but twin sons.

Grace in Loneliness

Tamar was lonely in her marriage. Perhaps her deepest longing was to be loved. She still had no husband at the end of our story. Neither of her two husbands had loved her. Many today believe marriage, or marrying a different person, will satisfy their emptiness.

The church is called the bride of Christ. *Church* refers to those who have been called out of the world to belong to Christ. Jesus chose you to be his bride. Whether you're married or single, you have the perfect husband in Jesus. (See Eph. 5:25–27, 29, 30.) He wants to nurture and love you completely. We can be as close to him as we choose to be.

Shortly after I married, an event reminded me how much I still needed my divine husband. I'd dropped Larry off at the airport and briefly left my car at the curb to help him with his briefcase. I returned to the empty terminal to find a big cop, by my lone car, writing a ticket. I told him I had only seen my husband inside the door and was back. "Too late," he said. "I've already put the date on the ticket. I have to fill it out."

On top of sending my new husband off for two weeks and getting a parking ticket, I'd just moved to Oklahoma City. I have no sense of direction, and I got turned around leaving the airport. Larry was barely out of town, and I was already lost. How would I find my way home in this unfamiliar place? Frustration stung my eyes. At that moment, I sensed God's Spirit nudging my thoughts.

What did you do before you married Larry when you got lost?

Ah, I'd relied on the Lord. Why did I think he'd left when I married? Tuning in to his presence calmed my emotions. I made it safely home.

As a single woman, I'd often leaned on God for help. After I married, I'd unconsciously transferred my reliance to Larry. It only took a couple of months for me to forget God's ever-present help (Heb. 13:5).

Wicked Er and Onan showed no concern for Tamar. Human husbands, even great husbands, may leave on trips or through illness and death. The worst in human husbands can't undermine the best in our divine husband.

Tamar reminds us that God's unmerited favor, not our worthiness or scheming, turns ugly situations into beautiful stories of redemption. She also shows us that we don't have to hide our ugly parts from God. As a perfect lover, Jesus sees all and still loves us unconditionally. What a big God!

Miserable beginnings can have happy endings for ordinary people who trust an extraordinary God. What mess have you fallen into or created? Will you acknowledge you can't fix it? Will you turn to God and trust him for what you cannot see today?

I Want to Remember . . .

Today's takeaways from #LittleWomenBigGod are:

Prayer Requests

Record your small group's prayer requests here.

When You Long for Unshakable Faith

Rahab means "broad" or "wide."

Rahab's slender silhouette filled the small window from which she drank in the night sky. Struck again by its order and beauty, Rahab remembered the stories of Israel's God. Fresh longing prompted an impossible prayer to the Hebrew God: "I want to know you."

FROM HARLOT TO HEROINE OF THE FAITH—RAHAB INSPIRES US. How could someone who began life on the "broad" path to destruction be heralded in both the Old and New Testaments for her faith?

Running an inn placed Rahab in the perfect spot to hear travelers' stories about Israel's God. She gasped the first time she heard how the Hebrew God overpowered mighty Pharaoh. She leaned closer to pick up the whispered rumors about a God who led and protected his people through the desert. "They say he appears as a cloud by day and a pillar of fire by night!"

The stories that caused her kinsmen's courage to melt made her own hope soar. The Hebrew God fought *for* his people. His ten plagues had defeated the many Egyptian gods and delivered his people from Pharaoh's iron grasp. How different he was than the Canaanite gods who demanded human sacrifices. When opportunity visited in the form of two spies, she was ready. She leaped for the narrow road to life.

Sometimes, those of us who have been blessed with Bible knowledge are tempted to assess our faith by how much we know rather than by what we do with what we know. Rahab had little personal knowledge of the one true living God, but at the risk of her own life, she put every bit of what she knew into practice. God rewarded her bold faith with a place in his Son's genealogy.

But Rahab is not without controversy. Some have criticized her methods. Was she wrong to lie? Does the Bible address this? I believe it does. You may be surprised at what we find.

Setting the Stage

Hundreds of years before Rahab, God promised to give the land of Canaan to Abraham and his descendants. Since God owns everything, the Promised Land was his to give.

Abraham's grandson Jacob, along with his sons and their families, went into Egypt under Joseph's protection during a severe famine. The Israelites, as they were later called, stayed in Egypt for four hundred years and grew into a mighty nation. Their numbers threatened Pharaoh, Egypt's ruler. He forced them into slavery and cruelly mistreated them.

God heard Israel's cry and raised up Moses to deliver her from mighty Pharaoh's ruthless clutches. The book of Exodus recalls this exciting story of deliverance. When it was time to enter the Promised Land, Moses sent twelve spies to check out the area. Ten of the spies returned terrified from what they saw. Their fear, like a contagious virus, infected the whole camp and erupted in murderous rebellion against God and Moses. Tomorrow we'll look at this misadventure.

Thirty-eight years after Israel's rebellion against God and failure to take the land, God raised up Joshua to lead the Hebrews into the Promised Land. As before, fortified Jericho barred their way. Our story begins when Joshua sends two spies to Jericho.

Jericho was a wicked Amorite city. It was walled and guarded. Their soldiers were trained and well armed. The Amorites were violent and evil, condemned in Deuteronomy 20:17–18 for the detestable things they did for their gods. They "frequently put live babies in jars and built them into their city walls as foundation sacrifices."[1]

Rahab practiced commercial prostitution in contrast to the religious prostitution that was part of the pagan worship of fertility gods. Her home, located on the city wall, was convenient for travelers entering the city. Enjoy the true story of a young woman who risked everything to pursue the one true living God and the life only he could give.

Day One
Faith Responds to God's Opportunities

Scripture Reading...

JOSHUA 2

MATTHEW 1:5
Salmon the father of Boaz, whose mother was Rahab, Boaz the father of Obed, whose mother was Ruth, Obed the father of Jesse.

Study and Reflection

1. Describe Rahab, including her qualities and line of work.

2. Consider the kind of company Rahab would have kept, the coarse conversations and experiences she must have endured in her line of work. What would you imagine her life to have been like?

3. How do you think the two Hebrew spies compared with the men she knew?

4. What did Rahab and the people of Jericho know about Israel's God (Josh. 2:9–11)?

5. How was Rahab unique in her response to this knowledge?

6. For what is Rahab commended in Hebrews 11? "By faith the walls of Jericho fell, after the people had marched around them for seven days. By faith the prostitute Rahab, because she welcomed the spies, was not killed with those who were disobedient" (Heb. 11:30–31).

7. The Bible calls the people of Jericho *disobedient*. This implies that they, like Rahab, had the opportunity to respond to God. From the following verses, directed to Israel in a time

of rebellion, what do you learn about God? "While you were doing all these things, declares the LORD, I spoke to you again and again, but you did not listen; I called you, but you did not answer. . . . I gave them this command: Obey me, and I will be your God and you will be my people. Walk in obedience to all I command you, that it may go well with you. But they did not listen or pay attention; instead, they followed the stubborn inclinations of their evil hearts. They went backward and not forward" (Jer. 7:13, 23–24).

8. What actions did Rahab and her family have to take to be saved from destruction? (See Joshua 2:17–20; 6:17, 25.)

9. Share your thoughts from today's reading.

Rahab Responded

Jesus said, "You did not choose me, but I chose you" (John 15:16). Jesus calls, and faith responds. God's Word is his invitation for us to know him better. The better we know him, the quicker we recognize his promptings in our day-to-day lives.

Rahab didn't have the benefit of Bible knowledge. Put yourself in her inn on the day the two Hebrew spies arrived. She didn't know them, and yet she recognized God's invitation and risked her life to save these men. Did she grill them with questions? Did she recognize something of the Hebrew God's character in these men that set them apart from the men she'd known? Rahab could not have created this opportunity. But somehow she recognized that the opportunity came from God and acted.

God knew what Rahab needed to trust him. He also prepares us for his calling. When he knocks, his Spirit nudges us to welcome him into our hearts (Rev. 3:20). Sadly, the rest of Jericho closed their ears to his call. God called them disobedient because they stubbornly resisted his revelation and invitation to faith.

The principle of responding to God's initiative applies to everyday life, not just salvation or adventures like Rahab's. God initiates, and we follow. It took a while for me to understand this. I thought I had to create opportunities to serve God instead of listening to his work in my heart and responding to the opportunities he orchestrated.

I was on staff with an organization whose founder, Dr. Bill Bright, had the gift of evangelism. He shared with everyone he met. He considered a short elevator ride to be a divine appointment to share the gospel. I thought if I had better faith, my life would look like Dr. Bright's. But I couldn't think of anything to say in a casual encounter. Or when I ran into a store, my mind focused on what I needed to pick up for dinner and not on where the clerk would spend eternity.

Tired of feeling condemned for my failure to meet my expectations on witnessing, I told the Lord, "If you put the thought in my mind, I'll say it. But if nothing comes to mind, I'll trust you didn't want me to share this time." I had this discussion on the way to get my hair cut. I'd wanted to share Christ with my hairdresser, but the worldly atmosphere in the salon had not been conducive. That day God opened a door, and I walked through. My stylist's concern for his sick child made our conversation timely and welcome.

I've learned faith isn't brazenly jumping out of your comfort zone for a thrill or to impress someone. Faith is submitting to God's leadership. It is praying for eyes to see his work and obeying his promptings. This glorifies God and is a lot more pleasant than being driven by guilt or religious rules.

Rahab reminds us faith is not measured by biblical knowledge or spiritual experiences. God is not impressed by pedigrees and social standings. He was delighted in a pagan prostitute who trusted him enough to act when she met his personal representatives—the two spies. Rahab's faith began by listening to the stories of God. It grew as she responded to God. Ours will, too.

I Want to Remember . . .

Write down any statements from today's lesson that will help you recall what God is teaching you. Let's encourage each other by sharing them on Twitter with the following hashtag: #LittleWomenBigGod

Today's takeaways from #LittleWomenBigGod are:

Day Two
Faith in What?

"When we heard of it, our hearts melted in fear and everyone's courage failed because of you, for the LORD your God is God in heaven above and on the earth below."
—Rahab, Joshua 2:11

Rahab heard how God had squashed mighty Pharaoh to free the Hebrews. Her heart, along with those of her fellow citizens, melted when Israel approached Jericho forty years later. But her fearful heart soon soared in faith.

While Rahab had only heard the stories, Israel lived each scene. They'd trembled between the Red Sea and the dust of Pharaoh's advancing chariots. They'd felt God's wind whipping through their robes and tasted the salty air. They'd padded across the dry seabed. They'd watched Pharaoh's pursuing chariots crumple under the closing walls of water. Who'd believe the faith of those who lived this miracle would be swallowed up by fear in just two years?

Proverbs 29:25 says, "Fear of man will prove to be a snare, but whoever trusts in the LORD is kept safe." God had promised Israel the Promised Land. Moses sent the twelve spies to preview God's gift, not judge God's wisdom (Num. 13:2). After he'd proved his power through the ten plagues on Egypt and the parting of the Red Sea, you'd think Israel would trust him. Yet, like we often do, they believed their eyes instead of God. Their fear of the fortified cities turned into rebellion and doomed them to forty years of wandering in the desert. Lack of faith robbed them and their families of four decades of blessings.

Now, forty years later, fear also drove the people of Jericho. Their hearts melted in terror when they heard the stories of God's deliverance (Josh. 2:11). While Rahab's softened heart bowed in faith, her countrymen's melted hearts stiffened in disobedience. "By faith the prostitute Rahab, because she welcomed the spies, was not killed with those who were disobedient" (Heb. 11:31). The word translated as *disobedient* means they refused to believe.[2]

Two examples—one of God's children, the other of his enemies—show how bowing to fear instead of to God causes disobedience and loss. In contrast, Rahab's faith sparkles against the dismal doubts around her. Today we'll look back thirty-eight years to the first time Hebrew spies entered the Promised Land and examine the danger of placing our faith in the wrong object.

Scripture Reading...

NUMBERS 13:25–14:12

Study and Reflection

1. The twelve spies agreed the Promised Land flowed with milk and honey, but their fears obscured the good they saw. Only Joshua and Caleb believed God would grant them success.

    a. On what did the ten doubters focus (Num. 13:28–29, 31–33, 14:1–4)?

    b. What did they ignore (Num.14:11)?

    c. On what did Joshua and Caleb focus (Num. 13:27, 30, 14:6–9)?

2. Israel had little trust in God after experiencing amazing miracles. Rahab had great faith despite her limited knowledge and lack of experience.

    a. Whose faith do you relate to more, Rahab's or Israel's? Why?

    b. What do you learn from this?

3. Contrast how Jericho viewed Israel in Joshua 2:9–11 with how the ten spies saw themselves thirty-eight years earlier in Numbers 13:33b. What warning do you see in this?

4. Israel could have said, "Since God delivered us from mighty Pharaoh, we will trust him to fulfill his promise to give us the land!" What has God done for you that you can recall when you are tempted to believe your fear instead of trusting him? Fill in the following.

   a. Since God did this:

   b. I will trust him with this:

5. The ten spies feared what their enemies might do to them. What fear taunts you?

6. How do we stop fear from sabotaging our faith and destiny?

7. James speaks of two kinds of faith. What is the difference between demon faith that shudders and Rahab's faith that stands? See the verses below.

   a. But someone will say, "You have faith; I have deeds." Show me your faith without deeds, and I will show you my faith by my deeds. You believe that there is one God. Good! Even the demons believe that—and shudder. You foolish

person, do you want evidence that faith without deeds is
useless? (James 2:18–20)

b. You see that a person is considered righteous by what
they do and not by faith alone. In the same way, was not
even Rahab the prostitute considered righteous for what
she did when she gave lodging to the spies and sent them
off in a different direction? As the body without the spirit
is dead, so faith without deeds is dead. (James 2:24–26)

8. Rahab had an unexpected opportunity to demonstrate saving
faith in God and be delivered from destruction in this life
and the next. Statistically, we have a 100 percent chance of
dying. From the following verses, what actions must we take
to preserve our lives for eternity?

a. For God so loved the world that he gave his one and
only Son, that whoever believes in him shall not perish
but have eternal life. For God did not send his Son into
the world to condemn the world, but to save the world
through him. Whoever believes in him is not condemned,
but whoever does not believe stands condemned already
because they have not believed in the name of God's one
and only Son. (John 3:16–18)

b. Whoever believes in the Son has eternal life, but whoever
rejects the Son will not see life, for God's wrath remains
on them. (John 3:36)

9. Have you accepted the deliverance from sin God offers through Jesus?

What Is the Object of Your Faith?

One year, our family lived on a small lake in northern Indiana right below the Snowbelt. My jaw dropped the first time I saw heavy trucks travel across frozen water. When we moved to Raleigh, my kindergarten-aged son remembered the trucks on the lake. He tried to scoot across a North Carolina pond after only a few days of freezing weather. Thankfully, he fell through at the shallow edge. Great faith in thin ice won't hold up a child.

Faith is only as reliable as its object. The thickness of the ice, not the driver's faith, held up the truck in Indiana. Rahab's faith worked because of a great God, not because of the size of her faith, the depth of her knowledge, or the breadth of her experience.

Have you ever thought, *When I have more spiritual knowledge and experience, then I'll boldly live my faith?* Thirty-eight years before Rahab met the two spies, ten Hebrew spies believed their eyes instead of God's promises. These men had personally witnessed God's ten plagues and parting of the Red Sea. The ten spies believed their enemy saw them as grasshoppers to smash. Yet when Jericho looked at Israel, they didn't see grasshoppers. They shuddered at her mighty God!

Physical senses are not reliable indicators of spiritual realities. We can't see God's power or plan with human eyes. God and his Word are the objects of unshakable faith. Those who trust in him will not be disappointed. These men measured their chances for success by comparing themselves with their enemies. They should have measured their enemies against their God.

Their lack of faith harmed the loved ones they'd hoped to protect. God closed the Promised Land to that rebellious generation. More knowledge, more experiences, and more time won't make passive faith grow.

Many things distract us from simple faith. We begin our journey trusting God to guide. Somewhere in our walk, we discover we've slipped into trusting *our ability* to hear. We trust God's promise to provide, but circumstances shake us, and we begin to rely on *our capability* to produce. In spite of our best efforts, feelings vacillate, negative thoughts attack, and our five senses redefine spiritual realities. Paul wrote: "I know *whom* I have believed," not *what* (2 Tim. 1:12; emphasis mine). Jesus alone remains the same "yesterday and today and forever" (Heb. 13:8). He alone is the unshakable object of faith.

I Want to Remember . . .

Today's takeaways from #LittleWomenBigGod are:

Day Three

Shaken Faith Reveals Our Foundation

Rahab's house on the city wall had been an ideal location for an inn. Now it provided a bird's-eye view of Israel's soldiers marching around her city. Did the hair on her neck stand on end when the priests blew their trumpets of rams' horns? Did she wonder if this would be the first day of her new life with the people of God? What did she think when they left?

Early the next morning, Israel's armies returned. Two, three . . . six days of the same routine: the priests and fighting men would come, circle the city, and leave.

Day seven began as the previous six had, but this time the circling of Jericho continued. Tension mounted with each orbit. The seventh time around, a long blast from the rams' horns and a loud shout made her stomach flip. Her home shook; dust stung her eyes and nostrils. Jericho's great walls were crumbling!

Scripture Reading..
JOSHUA 6

Study and Reflection

1. Imagine being in Rahab's home when the walls began to shake. Why would you need faith to stay put while the city walls fell around you?

2. Do you think Rahab's family gathered with her because of Rahab or because they trusted the God of Israel?

Shaking Away Doubts

Rahab reminds me of another woman with a sexually tarnished past. Jesus shook the woman at the well with his intimate knowledge of her relationship history. Her whole town wanted to hear more about Jesus because of her declarations about him. After experiencing Jesus themselves, the people said, "We no longer believe just because of what you said; now we have heard for ourselves, and we know that this man really is the Savior of the world" (John 4:42).

Rahab's family believed her enough to gather in her home. But after the city walls fell around them and Rahab's house alone stood unharmed in the rubble, I'm sure their faith transferred from her to her God. Sharing our experience with Christ helps those we love to trust him when their circumstances are shaken.

Study and Reflection

3. God saved all of Rahab's family who gathered in her house (Josh. 6:17, 23).

   a. How might, or how has, God used your faith to rescue family members and friends? Or, how has a family member's faith encouraged your faith?

   b. Ask God to reveal himself to those who hear your story of faith. The last chapter of this book will prepare you to share your story effectively with others.

4. Does God condemn someone who practices biblical faith but still feels fearful? Why or why not?

5. What would you say about the faith of those who feel confident in their biblical knowledge but don't practice the faith they profess? "For it is not those who hear the law who are righteous in God's sight, but it is those who obey the law who will be declared righteous" (Rom. 2:13).

6. Where are you struggling to practice what you know? Write a prayer asking God to help you trust and obey.

7. Rahab had to tie a scarlet cord in her window or the spies would be released from their oath (Josh. 2:18). What other biblical time were lives spared because of a red marker outside the home? (See Exodus 12:5–7, 12–14.)

8. Relate the scarlet cord to the foundation of our salvation. See the following verses.

   a. In fact, the law requires that nearly everything be cleansed with blood, and without the shedding of blood there is noforgiveness. (Heb. 9:22)

   b. For you know that it was not with perishable things such as silver or gold that you were redeemed from the empty way of life handed down to you from your ancestors, but with the precious blood of Christ, a lamb without blemish or defect. (1 Pet. 1:18–19)

9. Rahab said good-bye to her home, friends, and culture to follow God. We know from history that she would have lost these when Jericho fell, but her faith helped her recognize the value of taking this risk while living within her fortified city. What "walls" have provided you a false sense of security?

10. What has Jesus asked you to leave (or have you left) in order to follow him?

Jiggling Gelatin Planted on the Rock

When Jesus taught on forgiveness, his disciples said, "Increase our faith!" (Luke 17:5). Jesus said they only needed a mustard seed of faith. In other words, don't use little faith as an excuse for disobedience.

When the walls began to crumble, it was Rahab's actions, not her instincts, that revealed her faith. It doesn't matter whether her emotions shouted, "Run for your life," or if she marveled, "I'm part of a miracle." She and those with faith to stay in her house— the fretful and the calm—were saved. Biblical faith is not the same as feeling confident. Faith stands on God whether fickle feelings cooperate or not.

Courage, like faith, is not the absence of fear. It takes more courage to act when we are afraid. Similarly, faith is needed whether we feel hopeless or optimistic. It is normal for past rejection, betrayal, and trauma to generate negative thoughts and feelings, but we don't have to obey them. The loud crashing of Jericho's walls was the sound of God's victory for his people and Rahab. But to Rahab, huddled in her quaking home, it may have *felt* like her destruction.

Do you yearn for a day when you no longer feel afraid or insecure? Could it be those struggles are opportunities to exercise your faith muscles? Faith pleases God (Heb. 11:6). He allows situations that test our faith so we will experience him in fresh ways. Like physical muscles, the more we use our faith, the stronger it grows.

A dear older saint, who has faithfully walked with the Lord her entire adult life, suddenly faced new fears and challenges when her beloved husband of half a century died. Her fears rose as the sun set. She sang hymns to recall God's character and face her dread of passing the night alone. She grew stronger, but the fact those fears appeared at all surprised and bothered her. She came to recognize them as opportunities to experience God's comfort and presence.

Many of the lessons I've written about here later challenged me. I, too, had to refocus on Jesus and stop taking cues from the circumstances that taunted my faith. Struggles produce growth when we draw near to God and resist the dark enemies of doubt, fear, or passivity. Our enemies hide behind fortresses like the thick walls that protected Jericho for years. To free us from their influence, God must tear down these familiar strongholds.

Randy Alcorn wrote, "The faith that can't be shaken is the faith that has been shaken."[3] After our faith has been shaken and everything falls away, we are left standing on Jesus, the rock of our salvation. A trembling heart standing on the solid Rock is more secure than a boulder of self-confidence resting on quicksand.

I Want to Remember . . .

Today's takeaways from #LittleWomenBigGod are:

Day Four
Faith Is Our Compass

Larry and I arrived in Poland on the one-year anniversary of a bloody demonstration. Government officers had used AK-47s to open fire on peaceful demonstrators. The police had brutally beaten and killed many people. Soldiers holding machine guns lined the streets we walked on our first night in Warsaw. Hundreds of citizens carried glowing candles in a show of solidarity. The silence was deafening.

During our month in this communist country, I wrestled with issues I'd never faced in the United States. We went as missionaries, but we had to declare ourselves as tourists. One couple from our team had already been kicked out of another communist country for smuggling Bibles. They walked out of the country, leaving their van and belongings behind.

We staggered arrival times to homes to avoid drawing attention. On our last day, the militia hauled in one of the Christian Polish youths. They knew everything he had done with our group during the previous weeks. They roughed him up and sent him off with a stern warning.

Anti-Christian laws force Christians who walk with God into uncomfortable and dangerous situations. In ideal circumstances, children of God have no need for camouflage. Unfortunately, there are times and places when openness jeopardizes the lives we serve. Thankfully, the Bible not only teaches the ideal, but it also gives examples of how to function when life is dangerous.

In Rahab's story, spying, hiding, lying, and sending the Hebrew spies off in a different direction were all part of a deception to protect God's people, Israel. How do we reconcile this deceptive behavior with God's righteous character? What are the principles to guide us? Today we delve into the issue of honesty and who defines right and wrong.

Scripture Reading..

JOSHUA 6:17, 25
The city and all that is in it are to be devoted to the LORD. Only Rahab the prostitute and all who are with her in her house shall be spared, because she hid the spies we sent. . . . But Joshua spared Rahab the prostitute, with her family and all who belonged to her, because she hid the men Joshua had sent as spies to Jericho—and she lives among the Israelites to this day.

HEBREWS 11:31
By faith the prostitute Rahab, because she welcomed the spies, was not killed with those who were disobedient.

JAMES 2:25–26
In the same way, was not even Rahab the prostitute considered righteous for what she did when she gave lodging to the spies and sent them off in a different direction? As the body without the spirit is dead, so faith without deeds is dead.

ROMANS 14:4
Who are you to judge someone else's servant? To their own master, servants stand or fall. And they will stand, for the Lord is able to make them stand.

ROMANS 14:23
But whoever has doubts is condemned if they eat, because their eating is not from faith; and everything that does not come from faith is sin.

Study and Reflection

1. Why was Rahab considered righteous?

2. Some have criticized Rahab for misleading her countrymen when they came seeking the Hebrew spies. How does the New Testament assess Rahab? (See the readings for today.)

Finding Our Plumb Line

A woman from the sheriff's department spoke to our home-owners association about setting up a neighborhood watch. She suggested ways to protect our homes and neighborhood from robbers. Her tips included how to make your home look occupied when you're out of town and how to make it look like you own a big dog when you have a small kitten. In other words, several of her tips boiled down to deception. Yet, I didn't consider her ideas to be morally wrong.

In his excellent book *Biblical Ethics*, Robertson McQuilkin relates many forms of deception that the Bible condemns as well as areas where deliberate deception was condoned.[4] The following list includes some of the broader and often overlooked areas of deception:

- Lying without words
- Lying by using true words (as Satan did in tempting Jesus and the media do when misusing quotes out of context)
- Hypocrisy (wearing a false face to give the impression you are kinder, better, richer, poorer, or smarter than you are)
- Exaggeration (of results, skills, knowledge, or experience)
- Self-deception

Deliberate deception in any form, not just in using untrue words, is wrong in God's eyes *unless* he says otherwise. God's definition of right and wrong may counter our feelings or logic. Our feelings often deceive us. For example, since our new nature is patterned after Christ's loving nature, it is not hypocritical to show love to those we don't particularly like. We would be false to our true identity to be hateful (Eph. 4:24). The same can be said of being faithful, patient, and kind, even when we feel phony.

To fly upright, jet pilots trust their gauges, not their feelings. They know they can experience the sensation of flying upside down when the plane is right side up. To live upright, we must let God's Word be our gauge, instead of our feelings.

Does God Ever Permit Exceptions to His Standards?

In considering Rahab's use of deception to protect the spies, let's look at some examples where God sanctioned exceptions to his standards. Then we'll touch on how we can appropriately use deception in our everyday lives. The Ten Commandments say, "You shall not murder" (Deut. 5:17). Some interpret that to mean all killing is murder, yet the Bible does not consider all killing as murder. God even commanded some killing. Self-defense, war, and criminal executions were not considered murder.

Likewise, God does not consider all work on the Sabbath to be violating the Sabbath rest. The Pharisees in Jesus' day were wrong to say Jesus' acts of mercy on the Sabbath violated God's law. In Rahab's story, God instructed Joshua to march around Jericho seven days in a row without resting on the Sabbath. God was not breaking his laws; his higher principles were at work.

Does the Bible Ever Justify Deception?

McQuilkin believes the Bible justifies deception in three areas: inconsequential mutually agreed-upon social arrangements, war, and opposition to criminal activity.[5] To look at some pertinent questions concerning the practice of honesty in our everyday lives, please read the addendum following today's lesson. Now let's look at honesty as it relates to Rahab's circumstances.

Concerning War, Spies, Codes, and Criminals

We know that God sets the standard for ethics in war. Since he instructed Joshua to set a deadly ambush, which involved misleading the enemy, we can conclude God sanctions such covert operations as a part of war (Josh. 8:2). In fact, God himself set an ambush in 2 Chronicles 20:22. And his prophet Elisha deceived an army of Aramean soldiers (2 Kings 6:8–23).

God instructed Israel to spy (Num. 13:2 NASB). We call spies *undercover* agents because spying includes deception.

The Bible *never* supports sinful actions, not even for righteous causes. King Saul learned the hard way that the end does not justify the means (1 Sam. 13:8–14). God ripped the kingdom from him because he continued to disregard God's commandments in order to achieve his version of success (1 Sam. 15:1–29). The process matters to God. McQuilkin said, "If war is legitimate, then ambushes, camouflage, spying, deceptive strategy, communicating in code, as integral parts of war, are also legitimate."[6]

God not only allows such activity, he blessed the midwives with families of their own for resisting Pharaoh. And they used deception (Exod. 1:15–21). Today, police and FBI agents use deceptive activity to apprehend criminals. And to deter robbers, we turn the lights on when we leave to make it look like someone is at home.[7]

Do you remember the nuns in *The Sound of Music*? After sabotaging the Nazis' vehicles so they could not follow the von Trapp family, the nuns meekly approached Mother Superior, saying, "I have sinned." Were they wrong to help this family escape? In light of what we've studied, I don't think so.

I've spent time on this topic, because I've heard many people criticize Rahab. Since the Bible commends her actions, I wanted to look at why her actions demonstrate faith in God and love for his people.

If she had hesitated or shown doubt, would the soldiers have believed her? I hope we never face situations where our quick response means life or death for others or for ourselves. But if we do, I believe God would have us act decidedly. Double-mindedness paralyzes us and makes us unstable (James 1:5–8).

That is why we study God's moral standards now so we will know how to act in a crisis. He's given us his laws and examples to guide us.

Jesus demonstrated faith in God when he healed on the Sabbath. Joshua showed faith in God by obeying his orders to march around Jericho and not take the Sabbath day off. Rahab revealed her faith in God by diverting the soldiers from the hidden spies.

Romans 14 says there is room for Christians to hold different opinions on disputable matters. Since, "Love is the fulfillment of the law," the important thing is not to quarrel over them or judge those who differ from us (Rom. 13:10). Work out your personal convictions with the Lord (Rom. 14:22).

By faith Rahab acted, and God spotlighted her in the Old and New Testaments.

Continued Study and Reflection

3. What are your thoughts on today's lesson?

Addendum: Are Surprise Parties Wrong?

Is it wrong to deceive the honored guest in order to keep a surprise party a secret? Do I have to reveal my intentions to those who ask? Note the following examples.

Inconsequential Social Arrangements

Regarding inconsequential social arrangements, McQuilkin cites the following. In Luke 24:28–29, on the road to Emmaus, "Jesus continued on as if he were going farther." He waited for his companions to invite him to eat with them when he knew he would dine with them. In Matthew 6:16–18, Jesus told his disciples to freshen up so it wouldn't be obvious to others they were fasting.[8]

We practice similar deception in our social settings. When someone greets us with a passing "How are you?" they usually aren't expecting a complete rundown of our health and life. Such details are inappropriate for the casual greeting of a passerby.

Deception on the football field allows quarterbacks to serve their teams. The element of surprise is part of many games, jokes, and stories.

Revealing Our Intentions

Jesus showed us we don't have to reveal our intentions just because someone asks us about them. In John 7:1–10, when the Jews wanted to kill him, Jesus did not tell his brothers (who didn't yet believe in him) that he planned to go into Jerusalem.

Samuel feared King Saul would kill him when God sent him to anoint David as the next king. To cover his true purpose, the Lord told Samuel to take a heifer and say he had come to sacrifice to the Lord (1 Sam. 16:1–5).

Revealing My Past

Have you ever wondered how much you need to share about your past or some negative aspect of your life? Are you obligated to tell the person you're dating or your spouse everything?

Consider *why* you want to share. Is your goal to get things off your chest so *you* can feel better? Will the information leave this person with an unnecessary burden or heartache? On the other hand, will more particulars remove a secret that is coming between you? Avoid the vivid details of the things you feel you should disclose. If asked, be tactfully candid according to the nature of the relationship. You don't have to share anything with casual acquaintances.

The New Testament calls Rahab "the harlot" when it commends her for her faith. Paul called himself a "persecutor of the church" (Phil. 3:6 NASB). Both references highlight God's grace—not the unseemly past of the person. In choosing a mate or close friend, find someone who understands grace and knows God gives fresh beginnings to those who come to him.

God wants us to speak *truth in love.* Our words should give grace to the hearer (Eph. 4:15, 29). Some spouses have said they wish they didn't know the details of their mate's past. Being informed that their spouse entered the marriage with a stained sexual history was enough.

We should always make peace with God over our sins. Our lesson on Bathsheba addresses how to do that. Afterward, we ask God how much we should share with other people. We need to let God, not guilt, guide us—and faith, not fear, restrain us.

The person who is unmarried and feels she needs to reveal more information, or wants to know more about her intended spouse, should address those areas before marriage. She must let love be her guide, not dumping to find personal relief. My husband, who is a marriage counselor, says, "Be constructive, not cathartic."

Recurring Sin

What if your issue is persistent, such as sex outside of marriage, pornography, illicit drugs, or other addictions? If an issue has the potential to negatively affect your future, then disclosure is necessary. It is wise to allow your future mate to understand and shoulder big struggles and losses with you, and be warned of what he or she may be facing.

Many people promise themselves they will change once they're married. They don't disclose their current struggle with recurring sin because they fear the knowledge will sever the relationship. If past mistakes are "deal breakers," it's better to work through that now rather than live with a bitter, resentful spouse later. Jesus loves you unconditionally. Draw strength from his love and tell the truth in love.

The golden rule, "Do to others what you would have them do to you," guides us when disclosure is appropriate. We want to make our personal standards of honesty and integrity as narrow as the Scripture and as broad as Jesus.

I Want to Remember . . .

Today's takeaways from #LittleWomenBigGod are:

Day Five
Unshakable Faith Delivers

Someone described biblical faith as "taking God at his word." I like that. It describes a trust relationship with God. Rahab believed God would fulfill his promise to the Hebrews. He would give her city to Israel. Her faith directed her steps and changed her destiny.

Application and Reflection

1. What do you appreciate about Rahab, or how do you identify with her?

2. Why do you think God recorded Rahab's story and listed her in Jesus' genealogy in Matthew?

3. Apply this promise to Rahab: "For the Scripture says, 'WHOEVER BELIEVES IN HIM WILL NOT BE DISAPPOINTED'" (Rom. 10:11 NASB).

4. What did you learn about biblical faith from this week's study, and how are you applying it?

5. What do you learn about God from Rahab's story?

6. Hebrews 12:1 says, "Therefore, since we are surrounded by such a great cloud of witnesses, let us throw off everything that hinders and the sin that so easily entangles. And let us run with perseverance the race marked out for us." How does Rahab bear witness to the hope of a transformed life?

When You Long for Unshakable Faith . . .
Lessons from Rahab

Don't confuse presumption with biblical faith. Presumption has nothing to do with taking God at his word. It is based on wishes and false hope. It will harm you. Those who mistake presumption for faith believe God will rescue their careless overspending because God loves them. Or they justify marrying someone who doesn't share their moral and spiritual values. They trust God to "work it for good."

Hebrews 11:1 says, "Now faith is the substance of things hoped for" (NKJV). The Greek word translated "substance" is *hypostasis*. It means "a standing under, support."[9] Faith is the basis of hope. Faith in who God is and what he has said supports real hope. That is different from believing any random wish will come true.

Hebrews 11 commends everyday people who believed God. Noah believed there would be a flood and built an ark. Abraham believed God's promise to build a nation from Abraham's offspring. This isn't a list of visionaries who concocted spectacular plans. They were imperfect people who responded in faith to God's revealed plan.

The end of Hebrews 11 reminds us that many of God's promises are bigger than our lifetime. The ultimate promise—the heavenly city where all promises are fulfilled—is yet to come.

The Object of Our Faith

First Peter 2:6 quotes Scripture, saying, "He who believes in Him [Jesus] will not be disappointed" (NASB). A local pastor's wife visited the ruins of Jericho on her trip to Israel. Their guide pointed to one section where the wall still rises above the crumbled city. "Rahab's home," he said.

Rahab believed God would keep his promise and give the land of Jericho to Abraham and his descendants. All the faith in the world would not have saved Rahab if God were not behind the promise. Great faith in the Canaanite gods would not have rescued her, either.

God's hand demolished Jericho's walls. With perfect exactness, the same hand spared Rahab's home. The great hymn "How Firm a Foundation" reminds us that we are as safe as our foundation. Even if we feel like a quaking blob of gelatin, in Christ, we're secure.

How Firm a Foundation[10]

Verse 1

> How firm a foundation, ye saints of the Lord,
> Is laid for your faith in His excellent Word!
> What more can He say than to you He hath said—
> To you, who for refuge to Jesus have fled?

Verse 2

> "Fear not, I am with thee, O be not dismayed,
> For I am thy God and will still give thee aid;
> I'll strengthen thee, help thee, and cause thee to stand
> Upheld by My righteous, omnipotent hand."

Verse 3

> "When through the deep waters I call thee to go,
> The rivers of sorrow shall not overflow;
> For I will be with thee thy trouble to bless,
> And sanctify to thee thy deepest distress."

Verse 4

> "When through fiery trials thy pathway shall lie,
> My grace, all sufficient, shall be thy supply.
> The flame shall not hurt thee; I only design
> Thy dross to consume and thy gold to refine."

Verse 5

> "The soul that on Jesus hath leaned for repose
> I will not, I cannot, desert to his foes;
> That soul, though all hell should endeavor to shake,
> I'll never, no never, no never forsake."

I Want to Remember . . .

Today's takeaways from #LittleWomenBigGod are:

Prayer Requests

Record your small group's prayer requests here.

When You Grieve

Ruth means "friendship."

Naomi means "pleasant."

Elimelech means "My God is King."

Orpah means "stubborn or deer."

Mahlon means "sick."

Boaz means "in Him is strength."

Kilion or Chilion means "pining."

Naomi patted Ruth's shoulder. "You've been a daughter to me, but now you must return to your mother."

Ruth's tears had cleared her mind. She knew she could never go back to the life she'd had before meeting Israel's God. "Don't ask me to leave you. Please, let me go with you. Where you go, I will go; where you live, I will live. Your people will be my people, and your God will be my God."

WHICH HAS THE GREATEST INFLUENCE ON HOW WE TURN OUT? Nature or nurture? In looking at the women God chose to be in his Son's family tree, I'd say faith trumps both. Ruth was born of a race known for its hostility to the Israelites and, like Tamar and Rahab, nurtured in a pagan culture. Yet, she displays true noble character and exceptional faith in Israel's God. When our story opens, faith and character are about all she possesses. A young Moabite widow without money, food, or connections, Ruth has only her character, the company of her grieving mother-in-law, and her fresh faith in Naomi's God to support her as she begins a new life in a foreign country.

Ruth's story takes place during the time when the judges ruled Israel. Apostasy, warfare, violence, and moral decay marked this era, when "everyone did what was right in his own eyes" (Judg. 21:25 NASB).

Not only does Ruth live in a dark time, but her people had an appalling history. The Moabites were descendants of Abraham's nephew, Lot. You may remember that after Lot and his daughters survived the destruction of Sodom, his eldest daughter said, "Let's get our father to drink wine and then sleep with him and preserve our family line through our father" (Gen. 19:32). Their incestuous relationship produced a son named Moab, who became the father of the Moabites.

The Moabites worshipped pagan gods, sometimes with human sacrifices (2 Kings 3:26–27). They had even paid Balaam to curse Israel (Deut. 23:4). When that failed, their women sexually and spiritually seduced the Hebrew men (Num. 25:1–5). This brought disaster to the Israelites (1 Cor. 10:8).

If people were merely products of their DNA or environment, we wouldn't hold out much hope for Ruth's future. But Ruth will astound us with her choices, character, and destiny. But I run ahead of the story. Today we must walk with Naomi through her devastating losses.

Day One
Beware of Bad Decisions

Scripture Reading...

RUTH 1 AND 2

Study and Reflection

1. Just like Tamar and Rahab, Ruth is a Gentile from a pagan culture. Describe Ruth and Naomi. Notice their personalities, circumstances, and attitudes.

2. How long did Elimelech's family stay in Moab, and what happened while they were there (Ruth 1:1–7)?

3. Just as viruses are more contagious than health, so sin is more infectious than righteousness. The verses below show why God banned intermarriage. What happened when Israel mingled with those from other faiths?

> But they mingled with the nations
> And learned their practices,
> And served their idols,
> Which became a snare to them.
> They even sacrificed their sons and their daughters to
>   the demons,
> And shed innocent blood,
> The blood of their sons and their daughters,
> Whom they sacrificed to the idols of Canaan;

And the land was polluted with the blood.
Thus they became unclean in their practices,
And played the harlot in their deeds.
(Ps. 106:35–39 NASB)

4. When we're in pain, we want relief the quickest way we can get it. Knowing our unhealthy patterns can help us reconsider our actions before we make bad choices. How do you usually seek relief from pain? (Shop, eat, drink, talk, lie, sleep, pray, watch TV?)

5. What enticements can lure you into a "foreign land" or away from relying on God?

6. Running away from pain did not deliver Naomi's family from it. The plan to be away for *a while* led to family members marrying and dying away from home. Once we leave God's path, return may seem impossible. What finally prompted Naomi to return home?

7. When guilt and rationalizations anchor you in a distant land, what can motivate you to turn back to the Lord?

So Much Pain

In the previous ten days, Janice had celebrated her son's high school graduation—and attended his funeral. "The aroma of meatloaf, my son's favorite, wafted through the house. Any minute I expected him and my husband to walk through the door. Instead the doorbell startled me. As soon as I saw the policeman, I knew something had happened to one of them. . . . It was David. A freak car accident so close to home . . . now he's gone."

David was Janice's second loss. A rare childhood illness had taken her only daughter eight years earlier. Janice eventually tried to escape her pain by leaving her home and marriage. Suffering makes us susceptible to bad decisions.

In a few verses, Scripture describes another mother's losses. First, a famine uprooted Naomi's family and sent them packing for Moab. Our family lived in four states in four years. Even without the devastation of a famine, big moves involve loss—including separation from friends, extended family, familiar routines, and your place of worship.

Elimelech died sometime after the move. Naomi's sons, Mahlon and Chilion, married local women from a different faith (Ruth 1:15). Then both sons died without children. In this patriarchal society, Naomi and Ruth buried their financial security with their men. No wonder Naomi felt God had turned against her. Were these feelings exacerbated because she had violated a check in her spirit when they left Bethlehem or when her sons married non-Hebrews? Or were they a natural reaction to loss?

The Bible doesn't say whether Elimelech was wrong to go to Moab. Years earlier, Abraham, Isaac, and Jacob had in turn escaped famines by traveling to a foreign land. Their detours had tempted Abraham and Isaac to lie and claim their wives were their sisters. Their attempt to protect themselves had put their mates in compromising situations. But God also told Jacob to go to Egypt, so moving to a foreign land to feed your family wasn't wrong in itself.

However, the Mosaic Law prohibited Israelites from marrying Canaanites, in large part because of their idol worship. Perhaps Deuteronomy 7:3–4 (NASB) haunted Naomi: "Furthermore, you shall not intermarry with them; you shall not give your daughters to their sons, nor shall you take their daughters for your sons. For they will turn your sons away from following Me to serve other gods; then the anger of the LORD will be kindled against you and He will quickly destroy you."

The Moabites worshipped the god Chemosh, whose worship was much like the worship of the Canaanite god Baal. An article by *ad Dei Gloriam* Ministries on Ruth and intermarriage says, "One of their idolatrous rituals included child sacrifice."[1] A devout Israelite would not consider marrying a woman who did not share his faith. But being so far from home and grieving the loss of Elimelech, this hurting family may not have been thinking clearly. Or perhaps their wives showed receptivity to their God before the marriages were arranged.

The Bible doesn't comment on this. What it does show is when we wake up in a foreign land, no matter how we got there—God has left the light on to welcome us back home.

I Want to Remember . . .

Write down any statements from today's lesson that will help you recall what God is teaching you. Let's encourage each other by sharing them on Twitter with the following hashtag: #LittleWomenBigGod

Today's takeaways from #LittleWomenBigGod are:

Day Two
Make the U-Turn

On a trip, the late Dr. Henry Brandt, Christian counselor and author, said he once mistakenly took the wrong freeway ramp. When his wife questioned his turn, Dr. Brandt snapped, "I know how to get to Chicago." To his dismay, all the road signs agreed with his wife. But he kept driving. Miles down the road, Dr. Brandt finally humbled himself and turned around. Sometimes we have to make a U-turn.

Pagan Moab looked better to Elimelech than impoverished Bethlehem. Have you noticed how pain exaggerates the possible benefits of a compromising escape and minimizes the liabilities? The temporary detour from God's perfect will that we hoped would bring relief becomes a different prison that prolongs and complicates our agony.

Luke 15:11–32 tells the story of another person who left full and returned empty. This story is not about someone searching for basic needs but about a rebellious son who squandered his inheritance through immoral living. After losing everything, he was brought to his senses by hunger and a pigpen. He humbly admitted his sin and returned to his father.

His welcoming father represents our heavenly Father. If we need to return home because we have wandered away to escape pain or because we rebelliously stomped out of God's fellowship, we can take heart from this young man's story. Our Father longingly watches for our return.

Henry Brandt had to make the U-turn to reach Chicago. The lost son had to leave the pigpen and his rebellious attitude to go home. And Naomi had to say good-bye to Moab to return to Bethlehem. We too must leave our self-will to return to God. He provides the strength and grace for us to admit our mistakes and come home.

Scripture Reading..
RUTH 1:8–14

Study and Reflection

1. The path to healing often includes painful good-byes and uncertainty.

   a. What did Naomi have to leave to return to Bethlehem?

   b. Sometimes the thought of releasing an attitude, relationship, doubt, or guilt unnerves us. Who or what must you leave in order to move closer to God?

2. Jesus said, "Blessed are those who mourn, for they will be comforted" (Matt. 5:4). Grief can be displayed in many ways. How did Naomi grieve her losses?

3. Notice the relationships between Naomi, Orpah, and Ruth. Despite Naomi's sorrow, what kind of mother-in-law does she appear to be?

4. How did Ruth honor her dead husband (Ruth 1:8), and what does that teach us about how to show honor to deceased loved ones?

5. Why do you think Naomi changed her mind and decided to urge her Moabite daughters-in-law to return to their homes instead of continuing with her to Bethlehem (Ruth 1:8–9)?

The Not So Great Escape

We naturally recoil from pain. Sometimes fleeing our situation is appropriate. Other times, God wants to make us strong within our circumstances. An impulsive leap from a tree may land us in a thorn bush. Running away from unpleasantness rarely delivers us from pain, at least not for long. This is always true when we want relief *more* than we want God.

As often happens when we try to flee difficult circumstances, Naomi's and Elimelech's pain followed them out of Bethlehem and multiplied. The family had planned to be gone for only a little while. "A while" stretched into ten years. During this time, Elimelech died and their sons married Moabite women who served foreign gods. Any relief was short-lived.

After burying her loved ones, good news reached Naomi. "The Lord has provided food in Bethlehem." The kindness of God leads to repentance (Rom. 2:4). This news helped Naomi pack up what little she had and begin the trek home. The essence of repentance is a change in direction. Naomi left Bethlehem for Moab. Now she had to leave three graves, the relationships she had built over the last ten years, and her role with Orpah and Ruth. She had to say good-bye to the feeling of being in control. She had to let go and turn around.

I Want to Remember . . .

Today's takeaways from #LittleWomenBigGod are:

Day Three
Don't Let Pain Color Your Thinking

Scammers know people in dire circumstances are easy prey. During hardship, outlandish promises tickle our ears. Have you ever made a bad decision because you felt desperate?

The drive to escape pain distorted Naomi's judgment. In her grief, she thought it would be smart for her beloved daughters-in-law to secure new husbands, even ones who worshipped a bloodthirsty false god (2 Kings 3:26–27). "Go home and remarry," she told Orpah and Ruth. But Ruth had tasted the sweetness of the Lord. She wanted nothing to do with the dead religion she'd escaped. To be destitute with Naomi, under the wings of God, was far better than security under a pagan husband.

Naomi's bad advice reminds us that we must test even trusted human counsel against God's timeless principles. We'll never regret following his wisdom. It always proves sound. When we feel shaky, we must recall God's character. Focusing on our uncertain circumstances or losses only undermines our hope. Our security does not rest in how well our ideas turn out. Neither is it based on how certain we feel. God alone is the foundation of a sure hope.

Ruth didn't allow her losses to sidetrack her from pursuing God. If she could vow her devotion to her fallible mother-in-law, how much more worthy is our perfect Lord Jesus of our total surrender?

Scripture Reading...

RUTH 1:15–22

Study and Reflection

1. How does Naomi's advice to Ruth fly in the face of the following Scripture? "Trust in the LORD with all your heart and lean not on your own understanding; in all your ways submit to him, and he will make your paths straight" (Prov. 3:5–6).

2. Read Ruth's vow of commitment to Naomi (1:16–17). What does Ruth's vow reveal about her relationship with God?

3. Have you ever noticed how temptation presents a dazzling picture of the supposed benefits of sin? Yet when we contemplate a step of faith, all the risks loom before us. What is Ruth leaving in order to join Naomi and follow God?

4. How can you apply Ruth's vow to her mother-in-law to your commitment to follow Christ Jesus?

5. Ruth lovingly refused her mother-in-law's advice. What helps you recognize and turn down bad advice?

6. What do you learn from the following Scripture on how to gain wisdom? "If any of you lacks wisdom, you should ask God, who gives generously to all without finding fault, and it will be given to you. But when you ask, you must believe and not doubt, because the one who doubts is like a wave of the

sea, blown and tossed by the wind. Such a person is double-minded and unstable in all they do" (James 1:5–8).

7. Mara means "bitter." How does Naomi describe the change in herself since her Bethlehem friends last saw her (Ruth 1:19–22)?

8. Naomi was in an especially needy position.

   a. How did Naomi's losses affect her perceptions of God and life?

   b. Describe a time when you let your circumstances distort your view of God.

9. Naomi felt like the Lord had turned against her. What assurances do the following passages provide us about God's relationship with his children during hard times?

   a. What, then, shall we say in response to these things? If God is for us, who can be against us? He who did not spare his own Son, but gave him up for us all—how will he not also, along with him, graciously give us all things? Who will bring any charge against those whom God has chosen? It is God who justifies. Who then is the one who condemns? No one. Christ Jesus who died—more than that, who was raised to life—is at the right hand of God and is also interceding for us. Who shall separate us from the love of Christ? Shall trouble or hardship or persecution or famine or nakedness or danger or sword? As it is written: "For your sake we face death all day long; we are considered as sheep to be slaughtered." No, in all these things we are more than conquerors through him who loved us. For I am convinced that neither death nor life, neither angels nor demons, neither the present nor the future, nor any powers, neither height nor depth, nor anything else in all creation, will be able to separate us from the love of God that is in Christ Jesus our Lord. (Rom. 8:31–39)

b. And have you completely forgotten this word of encouragement that addresses you as a father addresses his son? It says, "My son, do not make light of the Lord's discipline, and do not lose heart when he rebukes you, because the Lord disciplines the one he loves, and he chastens everyone he accepts as his son." Endure hardship as discipline; God is treating you as his children. For what children are not disciplined by their father? If you are not disciplined—and everyone undergoes discipline—then you are not legitimate, not true sons and daughters at all. Moreover, we have all had human fathers who disciplined us and we respected them for it. How much more should we submit to the Father of spirits and live! They disciplined us for a little while as they thought best; but God disciplines us for our good, in order that we may share in his holiness. No discipline seems pleasant at the time, but painful. Later on, however, it produces a harvest of righteousness and peace for those who have been trained by it. (Heb. 12:5–11)

God, Do You Still Love Me?

My friend was moved to hospice recently to manage her pain. Cancer had spread through her spinal fluids and brain. Her bald head cannot diminish the beauty of her sweet smile. In a span of three years, Abby lost her husband and older son. Now she's dying. Abby has bravely clung to her faith through each jolt. She has peace for her future. But she's concerned about her twenty-seven-year-old son. He stays by her bed. Both know he'll soon be the only one of his family left.

To lose one close family member creates a hole that lasts a lifetime. To lose your whole family leaves a canyon. Three graves marked Naomi's losses. In this male-run society, her losses also meant poverty. Naomi's pain distorted her view of God. Do you know someone who is disillusioned with God because of severe loss? I remember telling God during an especially painful season of my life, "If you think this is building my faith, you're wrong! My faith is being torn apart, not built up."

In time, God allowed me to see some of the good my painful losses had brought about. None of us can fully understand a situation when we're in it. Some things won't be understood until heaven. But that's okay. God understands, and he's in control. His eternal viewpoint ensures he never makes a mistake. This is important to remember, because circumstances tell us the opposite. And our view of God affects every aspect of life.

I've learned loss and disappointments don't have to be huge to distort our perception of God. One summer, I planned to finish the coursework for a master's in biblical studies. I needed only three classes. I was packing some kitchen items for our time away when my husband approached me. He said our financial ministry support had been less than expected. The bottom line was that I would not be able to attend my classes that summer.

I was disappointed but didn't realize my sadness had polluted my entire outlook on life. One day, I sat on my bed and asked the Lord why I felt so gloomy. Immediately I sensed his response, *You don't believe I love you.* Shocked, I had to admit it was true. My letdown had poisoned my thinking.

Lord, I know you love me. You sent Jesus to die for me. I was amazed at how simply refuting the lie and affirming the truth restored my spirits.

When you can't shake a negative emotion, try asking God to show you what's going on. Give him time to reveal any lies you've believed about him, yourself, or something else. Has a loss affected your beliefs about God? Does God seem distant, cruel, or difficult to please? What difference would it make if you believed God loved you?

You can't imagine God loves you more than he does. He is love. Believe in his love. Abby did. I pray her son will, too.

Want to Remember . . .

Today's takeaways from #LittleWomenBigGod are:

Day Four
Do Your Part—Let God Do His

Jackie is a dog whisperer. She calls herself a dog trainer, but if you watch this four-foot, eleven-inch woman handle a 150-pound dog, you'd know what I mean. I wanted Jackie to help me train our five-month-old puppy, but I couldn't find her. I'd searched my emails and phoned where she used to work before running out of leads.

I do interior design work on the side. Every time I planned to visit the seamstress, something interfered. On a whim, I called another gal. On the way to her workroom, I again thought of Jackie. Imagine my curiosity when I spied a simple sign next door to the new seamstress's shop that read "Dog Trainer." A smaller sign in the window read "Jackie's Dog Training." Could it be *the* Jackie?

It was.

I marvel at my fruitless attempts to find her, my thwarted efforts to enroll in other dog-training classes, and the nudges to go to a different seamstress. God had not let my yearning for Jackie die. It took awhile, but at the right time, he connected our paths.

The mystery of divine sovereignty and human responsibility dances through Scripture. "The mind of man plans his way, but the LORD directs his steps" (Prov. 16:9 NASB). In ballroom dance, each dancer is responsible for his or her own steps. The man's role is to lead the dance. The woman's role is to follow. A subtle touch is enough to direct an experienced dancer. A new dancer might need a quick pull to avoid colliding with another couple on the dance floor.

Walking with God is a divine waltz of faith. It is not our job to lead. Our role is to stay aware of our partner and follow his lead.

God uses our needs to direct our steps. I was reminded of this when fifty robins descended upon my five holly trees and devoured the red berries. "Look at the birds of the air; they do not sow or reap or store away in barns, and yet your heavenly Father feeds them" (Matt. 6:26). God supplied the berries, but hunger drove the birds to search for them.

Faith does not mean idleness. Industry builds character and brings satisfaction. Able bodies that refuse to do their jobs sabotage their own character and happiness. Faith leads to action. Naomi couldn't toil in the fields, but she could shepherd Ruth.

Later, she will take on another delightful responsibility. But now Ruth and Naomi need food. Watch how God uses this ordinary need to accomplish his divine plan.

Let the Dance Begin

Boaz allowed the poor to glean his fields. He was also related to Elimelech. This made him a candidate to marry Ruth and buy Elimelech's land from Naomi. But how would this wealthy landowner and poor widow ever meet? I love how the New American Standard version puts it: Ruth "happened to come to the portion of the field belonging to Boaz, who was of the family of Elimelech" (Ruth 2:3). And Boaz just happened to be captivated by her!

Boaz, a kinsman-redeemer, is a type of Christ. (We will discuss the term "kinsman-redeemer" more fully next week.) He strode into his field with a heart bigger than Texas. Imagine working for a boss who blessed you when he checked on your progress.

Ruth probably didn't sense God's invisible lead that day. If she felt drawn to Boaz's field, she couldn't have imagined what awaited her. God used something as ordinary as hunger to direct Ruth to Boaz. He rewarded Boaz's generosity to the poor with an introduction to Ruth. Simple needs, a gentle prompting, and voilà—the hand of God.

Scripture Reading..
RUTH 2:1–5

Study and Reflection

1. From the following verses, describe God's provision for the landless, poor, and foreigner. What did the poor have to do to benefit from this provision? "When you are harvesting

in your field and you overlook a sheaf, do not go back to get it. Leave it for the foreigner, the fatherless and the widow, so that the LORD your God may bless you in all the work of your hands. When you beat the olives from your trees, do not go over the branches a second time. Leave what remains for the foreigner, the fatherless and the widow. When you harvest the grapes in your vineyard, do not go over the vines again. Leave what remains for the foreigner, the fatherless and the widow. Remember that you were slaves in Egypt. That is why I command you to do this" (Deut. 24:19–22).

2. Why do you think God wanted these people to work the fields instead of receiving bags of gathered food? See the verses that follow. "For even when we were with you, we gave you this rule: 'The one who is unwilling to work shall not eat.' We hear that some among you are idle and disruptive. They are not busy; they are busybodies. Such people we command and urge in the Lord Jesus Christ to settle down and earn the food they eat" (2 Thess. 3:10–12).

3. What motivated Ruth to look for work?

4. How do you see divine sovereignty and human responsibility working together to bring Ruth to her kinsman-redeemer's field?

5. Do you think Ruth was aware of God's leading?

6. Thinking back over your life, were you more aware of God's leading during the process or only later when you looked back?

7. Think of a time when you did not recognize God's involvement until after the fact. How does remembering his past protection and guidance provide encouragement for today's challenges?

God Uses Ordinary Circumstances

I didn't analyze the sudden urge to stop shopping with my visiting out-of-town cousin. I just ushered us to the car and headed home. As soon as we merged onto the freeway, Susanne spotted her husband in the next lane. He was lost. He and their children had been circling Raleigh without a cell phone. We attracted his attention, and he followed us home.

Have you ever had a definite sense of being prodded in a certain direction but had no clue why? Perhaps Ruth felt drawn to check out Boaz's field. I never would have guessed my impulse to start home would rescue my lost cousins. I thought they were at a movie on the other side of town.

Sometimes we mistake God's providence for bad luck. I'm sure that's how my friends Susan and Navaka felt when they weren't able to enjoy a beach resort on their vacation. In 2004, while visiting Sri Lanka, terrible stomach cramps sent Susan to the emergency room. Even with medicine, she couldn't shake them. Reluctantly, they canceled their much-anticipated trip to the beach. As soon as they changed plans, Susan's stomach calmed down. While they visited a nearby site, the beach they had planned to enjoy became part of one of the deadliest disasters in recorded history. Over two hundred and thirty thousand people in fourteen countries lost their lives to deadly tsunamis.[2]

God used an illness for Susan. He used hunger for Ruth. God uses everyday situations to propel us into his perfect plan. Sometimes we need the perspective of time to recognize God's hand. Have you felt abandoned by God? One day, you will see how his hand led you through this life. You will stand amazed.

God's story is not over. As with any good book, some things don't make sense until the last chapter. Until then, our role is to trust God with our disappointments. He is at work in your life just as he was for Susan, Ruth, and Naomi.

Want to Remember . . .
Today's takeaways from #LittleWomenBigGod are:

Day Five
Return and Be Rewarded

"I love you." Who tires of hearing affirming words spoken from a sincere heart? Some blessings need to be heard over and over again.

But words that aren't substantiated with actions quickly lose meaning. Boaz greeted his workers with "May the Lord bless you." He told Ruth, "May the Lord reward your work." He then ensured her success. He had her glean with his servant girls among the sheaves where she'd be protected. He commanded his men to pull out grain for her so she wouldn't have to pick up the trampled grain. Boaz supported his words with actions.

As you read today's passage, note the traits Boaz demonstrates. They make a good prayer list for someone who wants a husband. And don't miss Ruth's qualities. She has a quiet and gentle spirit that is beautiful to the Lord. She also has spunk. Bending over to pick up grain and swat bugs was the least of this young widow's concerns. In a time when each one "did what was right in his own eyes," Ruth would be easy prey for a ruthless man—or gang of men. After all, it was well known she had no husband, father, or brother around to retaliate for any wrong done to her. Ruth also had to swallow any pride. She didn't even have the status of a field hand. Some would have felt humiliated to be at the mercy of a stranger's kindness.

But God had prepared the way for Ruth. He had lit a spark in Boaz's heart with the reports of her kindness to Naomi and her faith in Jehovah (Ruth 2:11–12). When she showed up in his field, he couldn't help himself. He had to protect this rare gem.

Ruth and Boaz each displayed courage in their own way. Boaz boldly crossed cultural and gender boundaries to help this foreign woman, even to the point of serving her food. Ruth fearlessly risked rejection to ask to glean in a stranger's field and embrace hard labor. Today we begin their love story.

Scripture Reading...

RUTH 2:4–23

Study and Reflection

1. Gathering the grain the harvesters missed was hard work. How does Boaz show Ruth special attention and ensure a good reward for her labor?

2. Why do you think Boaz and Naomi were concerned for Ruth's safety as she worked in the fields (Ruth 2:8, 9, 22)?

3. How is Ruth identified in verse 6? Why was this characterization considered unflattering in this Jewish culture?

4. What gave Ruth her positive reputation (Ruth 2:7, 10–12)?

5. Most of us have things we would like to change about ourselves—thicker hair and more energy, please. Maybe you wish you could erase your past mistakes or injuries. Our character, faith, love, and attitudes matter more than things we can't alter. God promises that those who hunger and thirst for righteousness will be satisfied. What desirable character traits would you like strengthened?

6. How does Ruth serve as an example of how to respond to Christ?

When You Grieve . . . Lessons from Ruth

Like the morning sun peeking out after a storm, Ruth is welcome sunshine near the end of a gloomy part of Hebrew history. Her humility, sweet loyalty, and lack of self-pity set her apart in any age. Her life beautifully exemplifies our hope of God working all things together for the good of those who love him (Rom. 8:28).

Despite Naomi's longer history with God, she let her circumstances distort her view of him: "The Almighty has made my life very bitter. I went away full, but the LORD has brought me back empty. Why call me Naomi? The LORD has afflicted me; the Almighty has brought misfortune upon me" (Ruth 1:20–21). She reminds us how easy it is to redefine God based on our circumstances.

If she were full, why did she move to Moab during the famine? Often we don't appreciate what we have until it's gone. Looking back, living with her loved ones through a famine was full compared to being without them now. How easy it is to focus on what we think we lack and overlook what we have. When Naomi told her friends to call her bitter because she'd returned empty, she overlooked another asset. Later, her friends will spell it out for her, "Ruth is worth more than seven sons!" In other words, "Naomi, you didn't return empty!"

Pain and loss may lead us to conclude God is unhappy with us or he would not allow this suffering. That's exactly what Job's counselors insisted when Job lost so much. But they were wrong. On the contrary, listen to what God said: "Have you noticed my servant Job? He is the finest man in all the earth. He is blameless—a man of complete integrity. He fears God and stays away from evil" (Job 1:8 NLT). The devil slanders God's nature. He knows if you withdraw from God, you'll be left without comfort. He wants to isolate and destroy you. Beware of his lies.

God's character doesn't change with our circumstances. We must learn to examine life through God's character instead of judging God by our pain.

Trials show we belong to God (Heb. 12:5–11). God uses hard times to better us much like loving parents have their children do homework because they want them to succeed. If Naomi had been comfortable in Moab, we would not be reading her story.

A Redeemer Changes Everything

Boaz came from Bethlehem. His every gesture resembled Christ. Boaz cared for his flock and blessed his servants. This wealthy landowner not only invited the homeless girl to work with his staff but also personally served her lunch.

Boaz told her where to work to protect her and guarantee her success. He commanded his servants to take care of her just like Christ has commanded his angels to watch over us (Ps. 91:11; Heb. 1:14). What a noble man. What an awesome Savior!

Truth Delivers

Naomi's hope fluctuated with her circumstances. But we don't have to wait for our situation to change to experience hope. Jesus revealed the loving nature of our heavenly Father (John 1:14, 14:6–10). The secret to hope is to allow God's Word to define who God is instead of our emotions, logic, or the moment.

Whatever shortcomings Naomi and her family may have had in their expression of faith, it's clear Naomi knew and worshipped the God of Israel. She loved Ruth and Orpah. While living in this Hebrew family, Ruth witnessed their faith, experienced their love, and obviously hungered to know their God. She ultimately chose the company of her mother-in-law and her mother-in-law's God over returning to her own family and gods. She risked rejection and humiliation in a foreign land to remain under God's wings.

During Ruth's life, there were no phones, email, or even snail mail. There were no buses or trains to return home if her new life disappointed her. Her commitment was complete. No turning back.

Want to Remember . . .

Today's takeaways from #LittleWomenBigGod are:

Prayer Requests

Record your small group's prayer requests here.

When You Are Empty

Obed means "worshipper."

FAIRY TALES, WHERE HANDSOME PRINCES SLAY FIRE-BREATHING dragons to rescue helpless princesses, still captivate me. Perhaps these tales resonate because they portray redemption. They remind me of King Jesus, who fought the devil to rescue me.

Ruth is such a story. Ruth was a damsel in distress. Widowhood was her dragon, poverty its fire. Marriage was a woman's financial security during this time. Children added esteem and the promise of a future. Ruth had neither. From a human perspective, to follow Naomi to Bethlehem meant financial suicide. What self-respecting Israelite would marry a foreigner from a group who'd cursed Israel?

Ruth clung to Naomi despite these challenges. Meeting God had transformed her values. Israel's God was living and caring. To be single in a place where she could be close to God was far better than any material security an unbelieving husband might offer. How could Ruth ever return to the spiritually and morally debased culture from which she'd been delivered? Naomi's people would be her people, even if they didn't fully embrace her.

Can you see God smiling as his invisible hand guides Ruth into Boaz's barley fields? I can imagine his thoughts. *Ruth, because you've chosen me over a man and material security, you'll have both. You will have a husband who will love and care for you and a special role in my story.*

Ruth had no idea of God's plans. Boaz was not just gracious to the poor; he was related to Elimelech, wealthy, and single. Can you spell E-L-I-G-I-B-L-E? Being a descendent of Rahab, he also had a soft spot for foreigners.

Under Hebrew law, the land belonged to God and was divided among Israel's tribes. If poverty forced a family to sell part of their land, then the closest relative or kinsman could buy it back to keep it in the family. If there was no close relative, the owner who sold it could buy it back if he became financially able.[1]

Naomi hopes to use the law of the levirate, which we looked at when we studied Tamar. Under that law, when a man died childless, his brother was responsible to marry the widow to maintain the late brother's name and property. Their firstborn son would be named for the deceased man and inherit all his property. If there was no brother, then the widow could choose a close relative. The widow had the right to publicly disgrace this relative if he refused to marry her (Deut. 25:5–10).

This law protected the widow and kept the land in the family. It would also provide Naomi with a grandchild. The late J. Vernon McGee said the widow had the responsibility to claim the kinsman-redeemer.[2] Knowing Israel's customs and laws and Boaz's generosity to Ruth, Naomi dares to hope again. She and Ruth need a redeemer with the means, heart, and availability to rescue them and their husbands' land. Naomi concocts a gutsy plan. Will Ruth dare to follow her mother-in-law's instructions?

Six weeks and barley harvest was over. The harvested grain would be carried to the threshing floor located at the top of a windblown hill. Strong-armed men would toss grain up for the wind to whip away the chaff. After the grain settled, families would bring their picnics and celebrate the harvest. At night, the families would return home and the men would stay to protect their crop. They slept with their heads toward the grain and feet out like spokes on a wagon wheel.[3]

Our story picks up at the end of harvest time. With no more work, how will these two women survive? Another type of hunger will prompt the next step of faith.

Day One
Choose God's Garb

My friend crossed the Atlantic seated near someone who had choking body odor. Fellow passengers covered their noses in an effort to breathe. A bulky man jumped to his feet, yanked down his carry-on bag, and sprayed deodorant in the aisle and in the direction of the offender.

Naomi's instruction for Ruth to bathe sounds odd to us. Our culture expects us to regularly wash away grime and odor. Perhaps water was scarce during the famine years. A bath may have been a luxury. Cultures without easy access to water don't share our hygiene standards.

Boaz had seen Ruth sweating in the fields. Now she wanted to be more than a reaper. She wanted to be his wife. The time had come for her to dress for the role she hoped to play. She was not seductive. Her character and kindness had already secured his heart.

Popular TV shows reveal our culture's obsession with sex appeal. Relationships based primarily on sexual attraction endure storms about as well as cotton candy holds up in the rain. That doesn't mean Christ-followers should look dowdy. Look at the beautiful colors and patterns God chose for rainbows, flowers, fish, feathers, and fur. Dull and boring doesn't convey godliness.

A Show of Respect

Audrey Hepburn was the inspiration behind Jessica Rey's swimsuit designs. This designer and actress designed swimsuits to show that modesty doesn't have to compromise style.

I see respect as a guiding principle to appropriate dress. Dressing modestly shows respect for:

- myself—as God's child (Phil. 2:15);
- God—as his ambassador (2 Cor. 5:20);
- others—by not being offensive, seductive, or distracting (Phil. 2:3)

Dressing seductively invites the wrong kind of attention. God's children aren't needy. Our Kinsman-Redeemer loves us completely. Ruth lacked many things, but she wasn't desperate for Boaz's love or attention.

Some women fear male attention. They hope a frumpy exterior will make them invisible. Accepting femininity, instead of denying or flaunting it, shows respect to the Creator of genders.

Scripture Reading..

RUTH 3

Study and Reflection

Redeem, redeemer, and kinsman-redeemer all come from one Hebrew word transliterated in English as *ga'al*. A *ga'al* would act as kinsman-redeemer by marrying a brother's widow to sire a child for him, redeem her from slavery, or redeem land.[4]

1. How does Ruth 3:1–4 address a woman's desire to belong, be loved, and be well provided for?

2. Needs and desires remind us we need Jesus. Underline phrases that show how God wants to care for you. What does each verse mean for you personally?

   a. "For I know the plans I have for you," declares the LORD, "plans to prosper you and not to harm you, plans to give you hope and a future." (Jer. 29:11)

   b. The thief comes only to steal and kill and destroy; I have come that they may have life, and have it to the full. (John 10:10)

   c. He who did not spare his own Son, but gave him up for us all—how will he not also, along with him, graciously give us all things? (Rom. 8:32)

3. From the following verses, how do Naomi's instructions to Ruth (Ruth 3:3) relate to how we are to approach our Redeemer? "Come close to God, and God will come close to you. Wash your hands, you sinners; purify your hearts, for your loyalty is divided between God and the world. . . . Humble yourselves before the Lord, and he will lift you up in honor" (James 4:8, 10 NLT).

4. We've all met people who looked good until they opened their mouths. Their self-absorption or irritability wiped out their initial appeal. Where is true beauty found according to the following verses?

   a. But the LORD said to Samuel, "Do not consider his appearance or his height, for I have rejected him. The LORD does not look at the things people look at. People look at the outward appearance, but the LORD looks at the heart." (1 Sam. 16:7)

   b. Your beauty should not come from outward adornment, such as elaborate hairstyles and the wearing of gold jewelry or fine clothes. Rather, it should be that of your inner self, the unfading beauty of a gentle and quiet spirit, which is of great worth in God's sight. For this is the way the holy women of the past who put their hope in God used to adorn themselves. They submitted themselves to their own husbands." (1 Pet. 3:3–5)

5. Our Redeemer has provided the best "clothes" for us.
   Describe them from the following verse: "For he has clothed
   me with garments of salvation and arrayed me in a robe
   of his righteousness, as a bridegroom adorns his head
   like a priest, and as a bride adorns herself with her jewels"
   (Isa. 61:10).

6. In the Bible, garments represent habits. Even today, we use
   the term *habit* to describe an outfit associated with an action.
   Consider how a nun's habit and a riding habit reveal something about those wearing them.[5] Underline what we are to
   put off and on in the following verses. What would these
   habits look like on you?

   a. You were taught, with regard to your former way of life,
      to put off your old self, which is being corrupted by its
      deceitful desires; to be made new in the attitude of your
      minds; and to put on the new self, created to be like God
      in true righteousness and holiness. (Eph. 4:22–24)

   b. Put to death, therefore, whatever belongs to your earthly
      nature: sexual immorality, impurity, lust, evil desires and
      greed, which is idolatry. . . . You used to walk in these
      ways. . . . But now you must also rid yourselves of all such
      things as these: anger, rage, malice, slander, and filthy lan-
      guage from your lips. Do not lie to each other, since you
      have taken off your old self with its practices and have put
      on the new self, which is being renewed in knowledge in
      the image of its Creator. . . . Therefore, as God's chosen
      people, holy and dearly loved, clothe yourselves with

compassion, kindness, humility, gentleness and patience. Bear with each other and forgive one another if any of you has a grievance against someone. Forgive as the Lord forgave you. And over all these virtues put on love, which binds them all together in perfect unity.

Let the peace of Christ rule in your hearts, since as members of one body you were called to peace. And be thankful. Let the message of Christ dwell among you richly as you teach and admonish one another with all wisdom through psalms, hymns, and songs from the Spirit, singing to God with gratitude in your hearts. (Col. 3:5, 7–10, 12–16)

Lasting Beauty

Margaret Meyers was one of the most beautiful women I've ever met. The loss of two husbands and two legs didn't diminish her appeal. She knew what life on the prairie was really like. Her stories of teaching in a one-room schoolhouse entranced me. The hymns she played on her harmonica brought a hallowed hush to my spirit. Her beautiful soul, like a spreading oak tree, had grown lovelier with time. At her hundredth birthday celebration, Mrs. Meyers beamed and greeted me with genuine delight. She recited the Gettysburg Address without a hitch.

Mrs. Meyers was always clean and coiffed. But her attractiveness, like Ruth's, didn't come from her pearls and styled hair. Her gracious essence enveloped me like a delicious perfume. Her spirit captivated me.

Proverbs 31:30 says, "Charm is deceptive, and beauty is fleeting; but a woman who fears the LORD is to be praised." Have you ever noticed that fairy-tale villainesses are often beautiful and charming? They use their looks and smooth words to bewitch their victims and conceal selfish motives. Biblical beauty radiates from within. Designer clothes of love, gratitude, and gentleness replace the rags of whining, criticalness, and insecurity.

Sex Appeal versus Real Beauty

God created women to appeal to men, but using sexual attraction against a man is ugly. Designer Jessica Rey cites research where Princeton performed brain scans on men looking at women dressed in various levels of covering. The scans showed that when some men look at a scantily dressed woman, the part of their brains that deals with thoughts, feelings, and intentions shuts down. Analysts from National Geographic concluded that bikinis cause male brains to see women as objects or as something to be used, not as people to connect with.[6]

Kevin Fast left this comment under Jessica Rey's godtube video.

> When a man sees a woman scantily clad, his natural response is arousal. Women, on the other hand, are not stimulated by sight but rather by the smell of a man, the touch of a man, and the sound of his voice. Women also require more time to become aroused, men see an immodestly dressed woman and are nearly instantly aroused.
>
> If a man were to walk up to a woman in a public place and begin to whisper into her ear and begin to caress all of the flesh she has exposed she would not only be offended she would report his behavior and seek a restraining order. He would be marked by the community as a pervert and shunned. Yet many women today parade around in every public place dressed in a manner

that produces in men the same responses and somehow that is acceptable.[7]

I'm not sure how many men agree with Kevin, but he makes a noteworthy point. Because we're wired differently, women may unknowingly cause men undue stress with revealing attire.

Ruth did not seduce Boaz the night she slipped into the circle of harvesters. Boaz would not have called her noble if she had.

The Cost of Beauty

Americans spend billions of dollars each year on beauty.[8] Besides money, we invest time and effort to maintain our hair, skin, nails, and wardrobes.

Inner beauty comes at a cost, too. Jesus spilled his precious blood to wash away our ugly guilt and shame. He conquered death to give us a sparkling new essence. His sacrifice transformed us into precious jewels. Jewels must be mined, cut, and polished to bring out their beauty. Otherwise, to the common eye, they look like broken glass.

The process of refining costs us

- time to get to know Christ better;
- humility to learn his ways;
- practice to walk by his Spirit;
- perseverance to break old habits and practice new ones;
- faith to rest in his grace.

The payoff is transformation.

God has provided all we need to reflect his glory. Our past, our temperaments, and even our bad moods no longer have the power to hold us hostage. As we look to Jesus, he transforms us from the inside out. Some hope marriage will turn them into secure, loving people. Walking down an aisle won't change anyone into a selfless lover. Bathing in Christ's deep love and swimming in his grace transforms us into true beauties. Have you considered how your choices affect your eternal beauty?

I Want to Remember . . .

Write down any statements from today's lesson that will help you recall what God is teaching you. Let's encourage each other by sharing them on Twitter with the following hashtag: #LittleWomenBigGod

Today's takeaways from #LittleWomenBigGod are:

Day Two
Identifying Mr. Right

When I was single, I worried I'd never find my soul mate. I'd tell myself, *If only I knew he was out there, then I could quit fretting.* Unlike the women in Ruth's day, I had a career to meet my material needs. But that didn't stop my concerns. I wanted a life partner. Yet I was picky.

One man looked perfect—on paper. We shared common interests. He loved the Lord. But when he said he wanted to spend his life with me, I felt suffocated. I prayed, analyzed, and finally concluded if God wanted me to marry this man, he'd make me want that, too. I felt terrible the day I told him I loved him like a brother, but I didn't want to marry him.

The next week my husband walked into my life. He was my summer boss. He asked the most interesting questions. He took me to a baseball game and an amusement park—neither of which made my list of preferred activities. But he made me laugh and think—and he was enthralled with Christ. I enjoyed being with him even when we weren't doing my favorite things. When he asked me to marry him, I didn't need to weigh the pros and cons. I knew he was the one. We married before the year ended.

I'm convinced God restrained my desires for my other friend in order to save me for Larry. In the same way, he protected Ruth from following Naomi's advice to return to Moab. Choosing to take refuge under God's wings is practical. When I remember God directs my steps and supplies my needs—including my emotional needs—I find the courage to trust his leading.

Ruth didn't know if Boaz would reject her. After all, Moses had banned all male Moabites from entering the assembly of the Lord for ten generations. He'd told Israel to never seek their prosperity (Deut. 23:3–6). Ruth already marveled at Boaz's kindness toward her. Why would this man be interested in her? Yet her faith whispered, *Nothing is too difficult for God.* She decided to follow Naomi's instructions and leave the results to God.

Clean and perfumed, Ruth watched Boaz bed down for the night. When the snores of the weary men reached her ears, she quietly crept over to Boaz's feet and lay down. Through this symbolic gesture, she asked Boaz to redeem her: "Spread the corner of your garment over me, since you are a guardian-redeemer of our family" (Ruth 3:9). The Hebrew word *kanaph* used here for the corner of his garment is translated "wings" in Boaz's earlier blessing to her (Ruth 2:12).[9] Ruth in effect is saying, "Protect me under your wings."

The psalmist uses the same imagery in describing God: "He will cover you with his feathers, and under his wings you will find refuge" (Ps. 91:4). Today we look at how Ruth follows the Hebrew custom and law to seek refuge under Boaz's wings.

Scripture Reading..

RUTH 3:5–18

Study and Reflection

1. The darkness of night gave Boaz an opportunity to refuse Ruth privately. List ways Boaz showed Ruth respect and care.

2. An edition of *People Magazine* touted "The 100 Most Eligible Bachelors." Photos of shirtless and open-shirted men filled the article. I don't think Boaz would have made their list. Thankfully, Ruth and Boaz had better value systems regarding what to look for in a mate. Which of Ruth's qualities seem to particularly impress Boaz?

3. How does Boaz protect Ruth and her reputation (verse 14)?

4. What about Boaz impresses you most?

5. A husband is to love his wife *as the Lord* loved the church. From what you've learned about Boaz so far, relate his traits as head of his household with Jesus' teaching and description of himself.

   a. "Come to me, all you who are weary and burdened, and I will give you rest. Take my yoke upon you and learn from me, for I am gentle and humble in heart, and you will find rest for your souls. For my yoke is easy and my burden is light." (Matt. 11:28–30)

b. Jesus called them together and said, "You know that the rulers of the Gentiles lord it over them, and their high officials exercise authority over them. Not so with you. Instead, whoever wants to become great among you must be your servant, and whoever wants to be first must be your slave—just as the Son of Man did not come to be served, but to serve, and to give his life as a ransom for many." (Matt. 20:25–28)

6. Why would these traits be important in a husband?

7. Underline the traits of noble character found in the following verses.

a. He has shown you, O mortal, what is good. And what does the LORD require of you? To act justly and to love mercy and to walk humbly with your God." (Micah 6:8)

b. The commandments . . . are summed up in this one command: "Love your neighbor as yourself." Love does no harm to a neighbor. Therefore love is the fulfillment of the law." (Rom. 13:9–10)

c. Love is patient, love is kind. It does not envy, it does not boast, it is not proud. It does not dishonor others, it is not self-seeking, it is not easily angered, it keeps no record of wrongs. Love does not delight in evil but rejoices with the truth. It always protects, always trusts, always hopes, always perseveres. (1 Cor. 13:4–7)

d. Now the overseer is to be above reproach, faithful to his wife, temperate, self-controlled, respectable, hospitable, able to teach, not given to drunkenness, not violent but gentle, not quarrelsome, not a lover of money. (1 Tim. 3:2–3)

8. If you want to marry, or have daughters or granddaughters who do, prayerfully consider the important traits of a good husband. Make this your prayer list. It will protect you from being taken in by transient charm. Also, list the qualities you want to possess as a noble woman of God.

Weeding Out Mr. Wrong

Barbara Nicolosi said her mother continually gave her the following "Reasons not to get married: 1) Because you are bored; 2) Because you want to get out of the house; 3) Because you think you can save him; 4) Because you are curious about sex; 5) Because you are pregnant."[10] Here are five keys to choosing a great mate.

Character or Chemistry

"Should I date the men I'm attracted to or the ones with solid character?" My young client didn't think she could have both.

I believe you can have both. But character trumps chemistry every time. Attraction can grow, but character is hard to change. Looks alter with wear and time. And remember, the Bible says, "Charm is deceitful." The person we marry will affect us—and our whole family—for the rest of our lives. It's wise to consider where the character of the person we date will take us in the years to come. Let me illustrate.

We were building our house in Raleigh when Hurricane Fran tore through North Carolina. We climbed into bed in our apartment expecting to dodge the worst of it. We woke up to devastation on a level I'd never seen before. Seventeen large pines mercifully missed my son's bedroom while he slept. The foundation of the house we were building, which we'd so carefully placed between two large oak trees, was filled with a hundred-year-old fallen beauty.

We fell asleep sending up prayers for our neighbors in South Carolina, thinking we were safe. We awoke to crashing trees and howling winds, smack dab in the middle of Fran. How could the weather forecasters have been so off? We learned that, far out in the ocean, the hurricane had moved north—just a few degrees. A few degrees doesn't seem like it would make much of a difference. But a few degrees extended over hundreds of miles put the hurricane in a different state.

What is true for storms is also true for people. A few degrees off in character, extended over several years, can put people in a different state of being from who we thought they were.

Who is the person beneath the charm?

Relationship or Religion

Judith dabbed her eyes. "Luke partied in college, but I thought he'd settle down after we married. I told him I'd never marry someone who didn't go to church with me."

Some women's spouses attended church while they dated. Others even led campus ministries. These women wonder how someone religious could be so unkind in private. The warning in 2 Corinthians 6:14, "Do not be yoked together with unbelievers. For . . . what fellowship can light have with darkness?" deals with a person's essence, not his or her profession of faith. There is a difference between having a religion and enjoying a relationship with Christ.

The Pharisees, who were the religious scholars and Bible teachers of Jesus' day, were hyper-religious. They also reeked of self-righteousness and lacked the mark of true faith—love for God and people.

Does this person show evidence of a dynamic relationship with Christ?

Respect or Pity

Pity has caused some to ignore warning signs. *When he knows he's loved, he'll change,* they reason.

If we have to look for the good in a potential spouse or make excuses for him, he is a poor candidate for a spouse. We must deal with what is. Choose someone you respect instead of someone you pity and hope to shape.

Am I with this person because I think he'll change?

Insight or Insulation

A grandmother, whose family was suffering with her granddaughter through marital separation and probable divorce, called me. The string of offenses that her granddaughter's husband had committed rocked the whole family.

"My husband and I could never picture our granddaughter with this man," she admitted. "Now we know the rest of the family felt the same way. What if we'd said something?"

My brother-in-law did express his concerns over his daughter's growing relationship with a young man. Separately, he told his daughter and the man that although he cared about the man, he did not see him as a good fit for his daughter. He offered to meet with him in a mentoring relationship.

Both were disappointed, but now his daughter is happily married to a godly man better suited for her. This wise father had built a solid relationship with his daughter. He knew she ultimately wanted God's best. Proverbs 12:15 says, "The wise listen to advice."

Do I welcome wise counsel?

In Love with Him or with Marriage

Some people fall in love with the idea of marriage. The fear of being alone or the refrain "No one is perfect" blinds them to potential problems.

A spouse of noble character may be rare but worth the wait (Prov. 31:10). Don't settle for less in the person you choose—or in the person you become.

Am I trying to make Mr. Wrong right for me?

I Want to Remember . . .

Today's takeaways from #LittleWomenBigGod are:

Day Three
Seek God's Man

Cindy twisted the tissue in her hand. "I'd planned to break up with my husband when we were dating. Then I remembered David in the Bible. He had problems. Look at the great man of God he became. I knew that could happen for Mike." After five years of marriage and endless sessions with pastors and therapists, Mike hadn't changed—at least not in the way Cindy had envisioned. "Why doesn't God answer my prayer?"

Maybe you were taught to "believe the best" in people. Jesus said to be "shrewd as snakes and as innocent as doves" (Matt. 10:16). David was a man after God's heart before he had problems. When we get to the chapter on Bathsheba, we'll see he had a good core. Never choose a mate based on who you hope he'll become or on self-made claims.

Who is the person now? What is his track record? Would I be happy if he never changed? Do I trust him to lead my future children and me? Would I be pleased if our children became like him? Ephesians 5 tells a wife to respect her husband. That job is easy when she marries someone she genuinely esteems. Practicing discernment in relationships is godly, not mean-spirited.

When Larry and I were engaged, our pastor asked if we'd still want to marry each other if we weren't Christians. His question surprised me, but I got his point. He wasn't saying it was okay to wed an unbeliever. He wanted to be sure I loved Larry, not just the glimpses of Christ in Larry.

I understood why he asked that when I began to travel with Larry and visit ministry staff around our country. Some of the wives would confide their secret marital troubles to me. One woman told me she'd married her husband because God had told him they were supposed to marry. She wasn't attracted to him. But how could she argue with a spiritual leader's word from God? Since he was a Christian and was convinced God had spoken to him, she concluded her attraction would grow after they married. It hadn't. His annoying habits bothered her more, not less, after marriage. She was miserable.

Paul wrote, "There is one God and one mediator between God and mankind, the man Christ Jesus" (1 Tim. 2:5). We must learn to discern his voice. We must not let others manipulate us with guilt or fear. Christ does not treat us as puppets. When we delight in him, he shapes our deepest desires. We find ourselves attracted to his perfect will (Ps. 37:4).

In marriage, we want to love our spouse's personality, values, and lifestyle. Small irritations become magnified when they affect us.

Enter marriage with your eyes open. Afterwards, there will be plenty of opportunities to *love by faith*. We all have times when we aggravate each other and act ugly. But in marriage, we want that to be the exception, not the rule.

The following poem describes the traits that help identify Boaz's and any man's intentions.

We need to teach our daughters to distinguish between:
A man who flatters her and a man who compliments her,
A man who spends money on her and a man who invests
    in her,
A man who views her as property and a man who views
    her properly,
A man who lusts after her and a man who loves her,
A man who believes he's a gift to women and a man who
    believes she's a gift to him.
And then we need to teach our sons to be that kind of man.
(Author unknown)

The work of redemption is Boaz's work. Ruth can rest.

Scripture Reading...

RUTH 3:18–4:12

DEUTERONOMY 25:5–10

If brothers are living together and one of them dies without a son, his widow must not marry outside the family. Her husband's brother shall take her and marry her and fulfill the duty of a brother-in-law to her. The first son she bears shall carry on the name of the dead brother so that his name will not be blotted out from Israel. However, if a man does not want to marry his brother's wife, she shall go to the elders at the town gate and say, "My husband's brother refuses to carry on his brother's name in Israel. He will not fulfill the duty of a brother-in-law to me." Then the elders of his town shall summon him and talk to him. If he persists in saying, "I do not want to marry her," his brother's widow shall go up to him in the presence of the elders, take off one of his sandals, spit in his face and say, "This is what is done to the man who will not build up his brother's family line." That man's line shall be known in Israel as The Family of the Unsandaled.

Study and Reflection

1. Their city gate was like our courthouse. Legal transactions and public business took place there. How does Boaz handle the legal aspects of redeeming Ruth? (Ruth 4:1–6). What reveals his eagerness in the matter?

2. Boaz wanted to marry Ruth, but a closer relative had first rights to her and her husband's land. Why do you think Boaz mentioned Ruth's ethnicity? Read the following: "No

Ammonite or Moabite or any of their descendants may enter the assembly of the Lord, not even in the tenth generation" (Deut. 23:3).

3. How could being a descendent of Rahab have played into Boaz's willingness to marry Ruth?

4. Think of how awkward it would be for gentle Ruth to carry out the stipulations of Deuteronomy 25:5–10 in an all-male assembly of elders. When Boaz had a discussion with the kinsman-redeemer who had first rights, how did he act for Ruth and spare her embarrassment?

5. Sometimes going through laws and cultural rules feels like a waste of time. Boaz loved Ruth but knew someone else had the first right to her and the family land (Ruth 4:4). How does submitting to laws and protocol demonstrate faith that God ultimately controls the outcome? See the following Scripture: "Let everyone be subject to the governing authorities, for there is no authority except that which God has established. The authorities that exist have been established by God" (Rom. 13:1).

6. What do you learn from the following proverbs, and how do you apply them to your life?

    a. The lot is cast into the lap, but its every decision is from the Lord. (Prov. 16:33)

b. In the Lord's hand the king's heart is a stream of water that he channels toward all who please him. (Prov. 21:1)

7. Which of Ruth's and Boaz's descendants made Bethlehem famous? (Hint: see Matthew 1:17 and recall whose genealogy we are studying!)

Character Is Demonstrated through Kindness

Our nine-month-old standard poodle showed me what "sick as a dog" meant. I called Larry to give the vet's report. "Max will die if we don't do surgery."

"A man is kind to his beast. Do the surgery," he said.

When I said "I do" to Larry, I couldn't have foreseen all the times his character would impact my life—even to how we treat our pets! Proverbs 12:10 says, "The righteous care for the needs of their animals, but the kindest acts of the wicked are cruel." Kindness is an essential quality in a life partner.

It helps if a man is strong in Bible knowledge, but knowledge alone puffs up (1 Cor. 8:1). Kindness and a hunger for God reveal the heart. Does he want to know God and his Word better? Does he show the same character around his buddies that he does around your Christian friends? How does he treat the elderly, children, the sick, his parents, and restaurant servers? He doesn't have to be an animal lover, but is he kind to them? Is he generous with his time, talent, and resources? We get an idea of the health of the root by sampling the fruit.

Ruth and Boaz individually demonstrated love for God and kindness for others. Their noble reputations were their calling cards.

Today's takeaways from #LittleWomenBigGod are:

Day Four

Recognize God's Unfaltering Goodness

The realtor who listed our house also owned the lot we wanted to buy. He promised to hold it until our house sold. We scrubbed and decluttered to get ready to put it on the market. Before the first person had a chance to view our home, our realtor called to say he'd sold *our* lot to someone else.

How do you handle disappointments? I have to remind myself God is bigger than my letdown.

If Ruth had given birth during her previous marriage, the law of the levirate (Deut. 25:5) would not have applied to her.[11] The objective of this law was "to raise up seed to the departed brother."[12] The closer kin than Boaz could have bought the land without marrying Ruth. Not having a child saved Ruth and the land for Boaz. Sometimes we don't recognize God's involvement in our lives until later.

We had to wait a few more years before we found the right lot. But during the wait, we clarified what we wanted and found a better house plan and lot. God worked our realtor's broken promise together for our good.

Scripture Reading..

RUTH 4:13–22

Study and Reflection

1. Why was Ruth able to conceive now (Ruth 4:13)?

2. Boaz became Ruth's kinsman-redeemer. From verses 13–15, what kinsman-redeemer did the Lord give Naomi, and what will he do for her?

3. Naomi told the women of Bethlehem that she had returned empty. How do the women describe Ruth's value to Naomi (Ruth 4:15)? In Scripture, seven often represents the perfect number.

4. Where do you feel your life is empty? What blessing could you be overlooking?

5. What new role was given to Naomi (Ruth 4:16)?

6. Remember the state in which Naomi returned to Bethlehem. Hunger drove Ruth to seek work in the barley fields. Six weeks later, barley harvest was over. How has Naomi's life changed since we met her?

7. Remembering from where Ruth and Naomi have come, what lessons do you draw from their stories?

Great Is Thy Faithfulness

What do you crave—security, peace of mind, health, joy, a mate, a baby? When we feel hopeless, we tend to seek substances, relationships, and activities that temporarily fill our void. Later we feel more vacant than before. Naomi thought she was empty when she left Bethlehem, but in hindsight, she realized she had "left full and come back empty."

Ten years of lack, loss, and pain convinced Naomi God had turned against her. She felt forsaken by God and reasoned that a husband from Moab was Ruth's only option for security. Ruth surprised her by seeking refuge under God's wings and offering Naomi her companionship. Weeks after Naomi returned home from Moab, she experienced a 180-degree turn in her circumstances. Naomi hadn't returned empty after all. Her young companion proved to be a valuable asset. She not only brought Naomi food, she captured the heart of noble Boaz who rescued them both.

God abundantly rewarded Ruth's faith and dedication to Naomi. Ruth's story ends better than a Jane Austen novel. Ruth marries a noble man who loves her deeply. Naomi becomes a satisfied grandmother with a new life to nurture. Ruth's and Boaz's baby, Obed, will become the grandfather of King David and ancestor to the King of kings. What a spectacular story from our amazing God!

I Want to Remember . . .

Today's takeaways from #LittleWomenBigGod are:

Day Five
Enjoy God's Provision

Naomi was Ruth's mother-in-law from her first husband. Was Rahab also Ruth's mother-in-law? Matthew 1:5 calls Rahab the mother of Boaz. Rahab married Salmon at the beginning of Israel's conquest of the Promised Land, while Ruth lived at the end of the time of the judges. Some believe a span of almost three hundred years lies between Rahab and Ruth and indicate it is more likely that Rahab was Boaz's ancestor and not his mother.[13]

This does not make the biblical text unreliable. The Bible often uses the term fathers to mean forefathers. Matthew 1:1 reads, "This is the genealogy of Jesus the Messiah the son of David, the son of Abraham." It looks like this verse covers three generations. Yet we know many generations lay between Abraham and David and David and Jesus.

Matthew 1:8 leaves out the names of Ahaziah (2 Chron. 22:1), Joash (2 Chron. 22:11), and Amaziah (2 Chron. 24:27), who lived between Jehoram and Uzziah. It is consistent with the text to omit generations and for Rahab to be Boaz's ancestor. Whether Rahab was the mother, grandmother, or great-grandmother of Boaz, her life influenced Boaz. He shows extraordinary compassion for this young foreigner. God clearly wants us to know he provides a place in his family for outcasts. He chose Rahab and Ruth, who came from two different enemies of Israel, to be in his Son's genealogy.

"Providence" is a name for God. "Provide" is the core of this name. God provides for his followers, no matter how helpless or undeserving.

Scripture Reading...

MATTHEW 1:5
Salmon the father of Boaz, whose mother was Rahab, Boaz the father of Obed, whose mother was Ruth, Obed the father of Jesse.

DEUTERONOMY 23:3
No Ammonite or Moabite or any of their descendants may enter the assembly of the LORD, not even in the tenth generation.

NEHEMIAH 13:1–3
On that day the Book of Moses was read aloud in the hearing of the people and there it was found written that no Ammonite or Moabite should ever be admitted into the assembly of God, because they had not met the Israelites with food and water but had hired Balaam to call a curse down on them. (Our God, however, turned the curse into a blessing.) When the people heard this law, they excluded from Israel all who were of foreign descent.

ISAIAH 56:1–3, 6–8 NLT
The LORD says, "Be just and fair to all. Do what is right and good, for I am coming soon to rescue you and to display my righteousness among you. Blessed are all those who are careful to do this. Blessed are those who honor my Sabbath days of rest and keep themselves from doing wrong.

"Don't let foreigners who commit themselves to the LORD say, 'The LORD will never let me be part of his people.' . . . I will also bless the foreigners who commit themselves to the LORD, who serve him and love his name, who worship him and do not desecrate the Sabbath day of rest, and who hold fast to my covenant.

"I will bring them to my holy mountain of Jerusalem and will fill them with joy in my house of prayer. I will accept their burnt offerings and sacrifices, because my Temple will be called a house of prayer for all nations.

"For the Sovereign LORD, who brings back the outcasts of Israel, says: I will bring others, too, besides my people Israel."

Application and Reflection

1. Moabites were banned from the assembly of God.

    a. Describe the exception God provided in Isaiah 56.

    b. How does it apply to Ruth?

    c. How does it apply to you?

2. Boaz saw Ruth's heart for God and love for Naomi. He redeemed their land, delivered them from poverty, and provided them with security and an heir. According to this verse, from what has Christ redeemed us, and what did it cost him? "Christ redeemed us from the curse of the law by becoming a curse for us, for it is written: 'Cursed is everyone who is hung on a pole'" (Gal. 3:13).

3. What difference does Christ's redemption make for us? "Therefore, since we have been made right in God's sight by faith, we have peace with God because of what Jesus Christ our Lord has done for us. Because of our faith, Christ has brought us into this place of undeserved privilege where we

now stand, and we confidently and joyfully look forward to sharing God's glory" (Rom. 5:1–2 NLT).

4. In the book of Ruth, with whom did you identify most (Ruth, Naomi, or Boaz)? Why?

5. What do you learn about God from our study on Ruth?

6. What helps you most from Ruth and Naomi?

7. Write down what you are trusting Jesus to supply. Begin to record verses that speak to your thirst.

When You Are Empty . . . More Lessons from Ruth

Once upon a time, God looked down from heaven and picked one family to represent him to the whole world. The family grew into a nation of people. Their numbers frightened the king of the land in which they dwelled. The king turned them into slaves, gave them backbreaking labor, and began to kill their infant sons.

When God heard their pain, his heart broke. He sent them a deliverer. A great battle ensued. God defeated the wicked king and his gods. He brought his special people out so they could worship him. He gave them sacred commandments that held the secrets to life and prosperity. To break his commandments would break their hearts and ruin their lives, he warned (Deut. 28:15–24).

One small town in the new land carried a special promise. God said his own Son, the deliverer of the world, would be born in Bethlehem (Micah 5:2). Jesus, "the bread of life," would come from Bethlehem, "the house of bread."

Sadly, the special family of God turned their backs on their Deliverer. They broke his commandments—and his heart. The house of bread became barren. Hunger became a gnawing reminder of their folly.

Hunger is a strong motivator. God uses it to bring prodigals to their senses. It invites us to return to our heavenly Father who waits to cleanse and restore us. Daily hunger reminds us of our daily need to be filled with Christ. Hunger drove Elimelech from the Promised Land to a pagan nation. The promise of food in Bethlehem drew Naomi back home. Ruth's hunger led her into the barley fields of Boaz, where she discovered much more than a day's rations.

God made us with needs so we would need him. We weren't created to be self-sufficient. Hunger reminds us to eat. Emotional emptiness reminds us we need the bread of life (John 6:48).

How Do You Satisfy Your Cravings?

How do you try to fill your void when you feel empty or lonely? This persistent ache should remind us of the promise of Psalm 23:1 (TLB)—"Because the Lord is my Shepherd, I have everything I need!" And Jesus said, "Blessed are those who hunger and thirst for righteousness, for they will be filled" (Matt. 5:6). Like Ruth and Naomi, we can know joy and satisfaction in this life. But we must guard ourselves while we wait. Cheap substitutes for God's provision will ruin our appetite for Christ as surely as junk food dulls the appetite for nutritious food.

The first three women named in Jesus' genealogy were Gentiles. They display God's great love for ordinary women.

Boaz provides another picture of our Kinsman-Redeemer's big heart for us.

There's a reason we love fairy tales. They're pictures of God's story. King Jesus trounced the dragon Satan to rescue us when we were foreigners trapped in the devil's claws. One day, Jesus will take us to his castle beyond the clouds, where we'll live happily ever after.

I Want to Remember . . .

Today's takeaways from #LittleWomenBigGod are:

Prayer Requests

Record your small group's prayer requests here.

When You Are Desperate for a Bath

Bathsheba means "daughter of an oath" or "daughter of wealth."

Bathsheba knit her dark brows together and looked again at the two men waiting in her doorway to escort her to King David. Why had the king summoned her? Had something happened to Uriah?

"WAS I RAPED?" A SIXTEEN-YEAR-OLD GIRL ASKED AN ADVICE columnist. She'd run into her older brother's nineteen-year-old friend. She found him attractive. He kissed her. She liked it, but she did not want it to go farther and said so. They had sex.

"I kept thinking, 'Stop! Stop! Stop!' But I didn't say it. I don't know why. I felt scared and shy . . . I felt too scared to say stop. I felt stupid too," she continued.

"My mom's friend said I was raped . . . Was I raped? I don't want to go to the police. I just want to know the answer. —Super Sad"[1]

I wonder if that is how Bathsheba felt. Three generations from her close family served King David, including her husband,

Uriah the Hittite. The prophet Nathan made it crystal clear in his story about the incident that Uriah and Bathsheba had enjoyed a close and loving relationship with each other. She was probably in her teens—maybe early twenties—when David summoned her. He was fifty or more.

King David, her sovereign, was not just any king. He was a mighty warrior, a handsome poet, and a respected man after God's heart. He had the star power of a modern movie star, athlete, war hero, and Christian music celebrity rolled into one. This legendary ruler no doubt awed her. David was her shepherd. He had reigned over Israel approximately twenty years (perhaps Bathsheba's entire life) when their story began.

Second Samuel 11 records the infamous and tragic account of David's fall with Bathsheba. The rooftops of family dwellings were enclosed courtyards and used as part of the home's living space. David's palace was located at a higher elevation, which made it easy for him to observe Bathsheba in her private quarters.

"David rose in the evening." That could mean sunset or night. Perhaps the darkness emboldened David to continue to watch Bathsheba bathe. Job 24:15 says, "The eye of the adulterer watches for dusk; he thinks, 'No eye will see me,' and he keeps his face concealed." David was stepping onto the path of adultery.

Scripture says David's messengers took her. "Took" is the Hebrew word *laqach*, which means to take, get, lay hold of, seize, snatch, take away, or capture.[2] Imagine having the king's men snatch you away in the night. We aren't given her thoughts or the details of what followed, but the prophet Nathan lets David know God saw it all and relays God's perspective on what occurred.

When you read her story, I think you'll agree that considering the sorrow, loss, and shame connected with her encounter with David, Bathsheba's rise above this tragedy to become his esteemed queen is nothing short of remarkable. For those who've felt the searing pain of betrayal or the sorrow of losing a loved one because of another's sin, Bathsheba's story offers hope.

Day One

Can Good People Fall?

Scripture Reading..

2 SAMUEL 11

Study and Reflection

1. Despite the fact that Uriah was a Hittite, his name means "Yahweh is my light." Yahweh is another name for Jehovah God. What does Uriah's name seem to indicate about him or his family?

2. David means "beloved." Contrast the character Uriah and David displayed in 2 Samuel 11.

3. Some years later, a census revealed that Israel had over one million fighting men (1 Chron. 21:5–6). What do you learn about Bathsheba's husband, Uriah the Hittite, and her father, Eliam, from the following verses? "These are the names of David's mighty men . . . Eliam son of Ahithophel the Gilonite, and Uriah the Hittite. There were thirty-seven in all" (2 Sam. 23:8a, 34, 39).

4. What significance do you draw from Matthew's remembering Bathsheba as Uriah's wife? "David was the father of Solomon, whose mother had been Uriah's wife" (Matt. 1:6).

5. How did Bathsheba respond to the news of her husband's death (2 Sam. 11:26)?

6. What did God think about David's "secret" actions (2 Sam. 11:27)? What warning or comfort can you draw from this?

Everyone Needs Cleansing

David, why, oh why did you do this? You were our hero! Strong and courageous, you faced Goliath with a slingshot. Tender poet and musician, you wrote our favorite psalms. How could you fall so far?

If David could have seen where his sin would take him, he would have fled to the battlefield to avoid his temptation. We may not fail in the same way as David, but we all sin. And every sin is serious. It changes our futures. I'm sure that Adam and Eve could not have fathomed the consequences that would come from eating the forbidden fruit. God had set this particular fruit off-limits to protect Adam and Eve—and us. We, their children, still bear the consequences of their sin, as did David's family.

We all must be diligent to protect our walk with God. If David could fall, so can we. If God could restore David, he can restore us when we mess up and injure others. And he can remove the stain of sins committed against us.

I Want to Remember . . .

Write down any statements from today's lesson that will help you recall what God is teaching you. Let's encourage each other by sharing them on Twitter with the following hashtag: #LittleWomenBigGod

Today's takeaways from #LittleWomenBigGod are:

Day Two

Is Sin That Bad?

Power bloated David's ego. He was king. Who would dare question him? Bathsheba's pregnancy no doubt was inconvenient. Since David couldn't hold back his own renegade passions, he was certain Uriah would express his legitimate sexual desires for his wife. His wrong would be concealed. Everyone would assume the child was Uriah's. Or so David's twisted thinking must have gone. But no one gets away with sin.

The book of James says full-grown sin gives birth to death. That does not mean someone drops dead every time someone sins. David's sin caused several deaths in this story, but death has a broader meaning than the end of physical life.

Think of death as separation instead of annihilation. In Genesis, God told the first man, Adam, not to eat of the tree of the knowledge of good and evil, "for in the day that you eat of it you shall surely die" (Gen. 2:17 NKJV). Even though Adam went on to live for hundreds of years physically, he died spiritually the day he ate the forbidden fruit. God's removal of Adam and Eve from Eden graphically illustrated the distance sin brought to their relationship.

Physical death also brings separation. The deceased is separated from those who remain on earth, but he does not cease to exist. The body returns to the earth, and the believer's soul goes to be with God. That is why the Apostle Paul could say he would prefer "to be absent from the body and to be at home with the Lord" (2 Cor. 5:8 NASB).

Sin kills closeness and trust in our relationships with God and others. Perhaps you have felt the chilling distance sin brings into a relationship. Unconfessed sin can make God feel distant, another reason to acknowledge the fault as soon as we become aware of it so we can be cleansed.

Scripture Reading...

2 SAMUEL 11:1–17

2 SAMUEL 12:14, 18

JAMES 1:13–16
When tempted, no one should say, "God is tempting me." For God cannot be tempted by evil, nor does he tempt anyone; but each one is tempted when they are dragged away by their own evil desire and enticed. Then, after desire has conceived, it gives birth to sin; and sin, when it is full-grown, gives birth to death. Don't be deceived, my dear brothers and sisters.

Study and Reflection

1. Relate James 1:13–16 to David's fall.

2. How could a man after God's heart instigate the treachery described in 2 Samuel 11:14–18? Consider the following passage. "See to it, brothers and sisters, that none of you has a sinful, unbelieving heart that turns away from the living God. But encourage one another daily, as long as it is called 'Today,' so that none of you may be hardened by sin's deceitfulness" (Heb. 3:12–13).

3. Proverbs 28:13 tells us, "Whoever conceals their sins does not prosper, but the one who confesses and renounces them finds mercy."

   a. At what point in a fall is the best time to come clean?

   b. What happens when we try to cover up our sins?

4. Not all attempts to hide our guilt are cruel. Sometimes we cover our sins with gifts or good behavior. Sometimes we cast blame or justify our actions.

   a. How have you tried, or seen others attempt, to cover up sin?

   b. What is the difference between confessing, or saying "I did it," versus saying, "I'm sorry you feel that way"?

Nobody Gets Away with Sin

Sin harms innocent people as well as the wrongdoer. It is simply not true that no one will know or get hurt when we sin. Tomorrow we will look at how to escape the seduction of temptation.

I Want to Remember . . .

Today's takeaways from #LittleWomenBigGod are:

Day Three

How Can We Escape Sin's Snare?

David could have stopped many times before his plunge into the abyss of sin. If he'd been at war with his army as his kingly duty demanded, he wouldn't have been tempted in the first place. But David stayed home. He also

- continued to watch Bathsheba bathe;
- inquired about her;
- sent for Bathsheba;
- lay with her;
- tried to cover his wrong;
- had Uriah murdered.

Oh, that he would have been where he was supposed to be or at least stopped in the early stages!

God *always* provides an escape from temptation. The earlier the exit, the less complicated the route and the less regret we'll face. But no matter how deep in sin we've gone, it is still better to turn back to God and 'fess up than to attempt to hide our fall with more wrong. God will help us face our consequences and cleanse us *when* we return to him.

Scripture Reading...

2 SAMUEL 11:1–16

Study and Reflection

1. According to the following verse, what does God promise to provide when we are tempted? "No temptation has overtaken you except what is common to mankind. And God is faithful; he will not let you be tempted beyond what you can bear. But when you are tempted, he will also provide a way out so that you can endure it" (1 Cor. 10:13).

2. Suggest ways to escape each downward step in David's great fall, from staying home from war to the letter sent to Joab (2 Sam. 11:1–16).

3. David became more ensnared with each step he took.

   a. Do you think David ever imagined his path would lead to cold-blooded murder of one of his loyal mighty men?

   b. What do you learn from this?

4. What warning do the following verses give against obeying your sinful desires?

    a. Jesus replied, "Very truly I tell you, everyone who sins is a slave to sin." (John 8:34)

    b. Don't you realize that you can choose your own master? You can choose sin (with death) or else obedience (with acquittal). The one to whom you offer yourself—he will take you and be your master, and you will be his slave. (Rom. 6:16 TLB)

5. When David took Bathsheba from her home to indulge his lusts, he was at the pinnacle of his career. He had success, fame, fortune, and power. He seemed untouchable. What warning do you take from the following verses?

    a. These things happened to them as examples and were written down as warnings for us, on whom the culmination of the ages has come. So, if you think you are standing firm, be careful that you don't fall! (1 Cor. 10:11–12)

    b. You may be sure that your sin will find you out. (Num. 32:23)

6. What hope do you draw from the following? "For we do not have a high priest who is unable to empathize with our weaknesses, but we have one who has been tempted in every way, just as we are—yet he did not sin. Let us then approach God's throne of grace with confidence, so that we may receive mercy and find grace to help us in our time of need" (Heb. 4:15–16).

7. From the following, what is our part in escaping the tyranny of sin? "Just as you used to offer yourselves as slaves to impurity and to ever-increasing wickedness, so now offer yourselves as slaves to righteousness leading to holiness. When you were slaves to sin, you were free from the control of righteousness. What benefit did you reap at that time from the things you are now ashamed of? Those things result in death!" (Rom. 6:19–21).

Our High Priest Gives Grace

When we give in to temptation, we give sin more control in our lives. Before we know it, we have become its puppet. But there is hope. When we obey Christ, we give him more control. The more we obey him, the easier it is to resist sin and do right.

Jesus was tempted more than any of us. He sweat blood in his struggle to resist sin. And he was victorious! He stayed on the cross when he could have come down at any time. He paid the penalty for our sins. He overcame death.

When you are tempted, don't run away from God; run to him. He'll help you resist. When you fail, run to him; he'll cleanse you. He'll never leave you when you're struggling or after you've messed up. Draw near to him, resist the temptation, and find the grace you need.

I Want to Remember . . .

Today's takeaways from #LittleWomenBigGod are:

Day Four

Is God Fooled?

There is nothing concealed that will not be disclosed,
or hidden that will not be made known.

—Matthew 10:26

Nobody, not even a powerful king, gets away with sin. Because God loves his children, he exposes our sin and makes us face it. This is a severe mercy to deliver us from its grip. How we respond to exposure speaks volumes about the true condition of our hearts. Notice how David responds when the prophet confronts him.

Scripture Reading..

2 SAMUEL 12:1–15

Study and Reflection

1. Which characters in Nathan's story represent David, Bathsheba, and Uriah?

2. Describe the relationship between the poor man and his only little ewe lamb (2 Sam. 12:3).

3. What does this comparison suggest about Uriah's relationship with Bathsheba?

4. Based on Nathan's account, what blame does God give Bathsheba in what occurred? Is she portrayed as a perpetrator, an accomplice, or a victim?

5. According to verses 7–10, who did God hold responsible?

6. Analogies are word pictures that help us understand a situation. How did Nathan's story explain the events in 2 Samuel 11:1–27?

7. How does Nathan show that God cared about David's pleasure as well as his needs (2 Sam. 12:7–8)?

8. In Israel's history, a king thought nothing of throwing a prophet into a dungeon if he didn't like the prophet's words. What does David's response to Nathan's words—"You are the man!"—reveal about David (2 Sam. 12:13)?

Speed Signs and Prophets

I tend to drive fast. I want to obey the speed limit and think I am—until I come upon one of those parked signs flashing your speed in giant numbers. I hit the brakes and look for a police officer.

Good drivers speed when they aren't conscientious, and good people sin when they're out of fellowship with God. Speed signs and God's Word show us when we're out of bounds to get us back on track. A wise soul heeds the warning and reaps the benefit.

Today's takeaways from #LittleWomenBigGod are:

Day Five

How Can a Dirty Conscience Be Cleansed?

Are you taunted by your past mistakes? Or do you feel damaged because of someone's sin against you? David's fall and recovery both warn and instruct us. A man or woman after God's heart can fall. But he or she can also be restored.

David was not an evil man. He was a good man who allowed visiting lust temporary control. His fall brought devastating consequences to many. But his true nature returned when he was confronted with his sins. His response to exposure set the course for his future. Like David, we can be cleansed of our sins, no matter how horrible they were. Like Bathsheba, we can be cleansed from sins committed against us.

Scripture Reading

2 SAMUEL 12:13, 16

PSALM 32:1–5 ESV
Blessed is the one whose transgression is forgiven, whose sin is covered. Blessed is the man against whom the LORD counts no iniquity, and in whose spirit there is no deceit. For when I kept silent, my bones wasted away through my groaning all day long. For day and night your hand was heavy upon me; my strength was dried up as by the heat of summer. I acknowledged my sin

to you, and I did not cover my iniquity; I said, "I will confess my transgressions to the LORD," and you forgave the iniquity of my sin.

Study and Reflection

1. In Psalm 32, David expresses relief over being cleansed from his sin.

   a. How does David describe his life while he suppressed his sin?

   b. What is the difference between confessing and suppressing our sin?

2. Relate David to the following verses. How can you tell if a "fall" reflects someone's true character or if it is a deviation from his normal behavior?

   a. For though the righteous fall seven times, they rise again, but the wicked stumble when calamity strikes. (Prov. 24:16)

   b. You can identify them by their fruit, that is, by the way they act. Can you pick grapes from thornbushes, or figs from thistles? . . . Yes, just as you can identify a tree by its fruit, so you can identify people by their actions. (Matt. 7:16, 20 NLT)

c. As a dog returns to its vomit, so fools repeat their folly. (Prov. 26:11)

3. What does the following reveal about God's forgiveness? "As far as the east is from the west, so far has he removed our transgressions from us" (Ps. 103:12).

4. What do you think this means? God blots out our sins *for his own sake.* Relate this to someone you've forgiven and with whom you want a restored relationship. "I, even I, am he who blots out your transgressions, for my own sake, and remembers your sins no more" (Isa. 43:25).

5. In spite of David's terrible fall, how is he remembered in the following verses? "After removing Saul, he made David their king. God testified concerning him: 'I have found David son of Jesse, a man after my own heart; he will do everything I want him to do.' From this man's descendants God has brought to Israel the Savior Jesus, as he promised" (Acts 13:22–23).

6. How do you apply today's lesson to your life?

When You Are Desperate for a Bath . . . Lessons from Bathsheba

Carrie's strained face revealed her misery. Long before we met, she'd fallen into an illicit relationship. Quickly, her guilt-stricken conscience forced her to end the affair. Yet, years later, she was unable to bear her guilt.

What do you do with guilt? Can anything really remove sin's ugly stain? David found cleansing. So can we.

First John 1:9 promises, "If we confess our sins, he is faithful and just and will forgive us our sins and purify us from all unrighteousness." Does this also apply to the self-reproach and shame that come from having been victimized? Can a victim be cleansed of sins committed against her?

At some point after the terrible event in Bathsheba's story, both she and David became aware of the stain of sin. Sin affects both victim and perpetrator. Victims of rape or exploitation often feel dirty, damaged, and even responsible for the sins committed against them. They blame themselves and replay the what-ifs in their minds.

Am I Soiled?

Nina revealed misplaced responsibility at her first confession. Raised Catholic, she told the priest she'd committed adultery. She was seven years old. Of course Nina hadn't committed adultery, but the adolescent boy who babysat her had molested her. She mistakenly concluded that since what had happened was wrong, she must be guilty.

Sadly, not just children draw these verdicts. It's not unusual for tongues to wag, "I wonder what she did to bring this on." If the slightest shadow can be cast on the victim, then the bystander feels protected from falling prey to a similar tragedy.

To make matters worse, some people don't know what to do with a victim. Bathsheba lived among David's other wives, concubines, and servants. Those who knew and loved David didn't want to believe he'd initiated such evil. It would be easy to blame Bathsheba to protect David and preserve their own comfort in relating to him. Victims face an identity crisis not only because of the traumatic event but because people treat them differently.

To be linked to a sin is not the same as being guilty of it. Jesus was a part of an illegal trial where he was beaten and mocked. Was Jesus' purity tainted by the wrongs he experienced? No! His blamelessness shone bright against their dark deeds. Bad things happen to innocent people—people like Nina, Bathsheba, and Jesus.

Can God Cleanse the Victim from Sin's Stain?

No one doubts David's psalms on God's cleansing applied to him, the wrongdoer. If the perpetrator can be cleansed, how much more can victims be washed clean? God is able to remove the red stain of sin—whether done by us or to us. "'Come now, let us settle the matter,' says the LORD. 'Though your sins are like scarlet, they shall be as white as snow'" (Isa. 1:18). From scarlet red to snow white—that's clean!

I remember how dingy my white poodle Pepper looked after a rare snow dusting in Savannah. White fur looks dirty yellow next to fresh-fallen snow. It's no accident God uses snow to illustrate the power of his cleansing.

At the cross, Jesus' blood provided our cleansing. He became sin that we might become the righteousness of God in him (2 Cor. 5:21). When God looks at a Christian, he sees Christ's righteousness.

When we, by faith, accept the death, burial, and resurrection of Jesus, we are identified with his victory over sin. The penalty for guilt was fully paid at the cross. Christ's work is greater than any sin done by or to us. His red blood washed away the red stain of sin and left us white as snow.

Why Do We Confess?

Since our sins were washed away, you may wonder why Christians need to confess their sins. Let's return to Carrie's story for understanding.

Carrie repeatedly admitted her adultery to God, but guilt still consumed her. Why? "Confess" is the Greek word *homologeo*, which means "to say the same thing as another," or "to agree with another."[3]

To confess our sin means to agree with what God says about our sin. We confess to realign our hearts with his and to restore our fellowship.

How Do We Confess?

Before we can experience relief from guilt, we must agree with God in two areas concerning our sin. First, we agree our wrong was wrong. Too often we avoid this. We soften our sin with nice labels. A lie becomes a half-truth; adultery becomes an affair; an abortion becomes a choice.

Sometimes we deflect and blame others. "If she hadn't provoked me . . ." Or we hide our sin under thoughtful gestures even though Proverbs 28:13 warns, "Whoever conceals their sins does not prosper."

At the heart of all sin is a wicked pride that we know better than God. God says sin is serious—to confess is to agree with him.

Secondly, we agree that Jesus' death paid for our sin (Col. 1:22; Heb. 7:27, 8:12, 10:12–14). Carrie had agreed her adultery was wrong. She had accepted responsibility for her participation and ended the relationship. But she hadn't confessed Christ's death had covered it.

I drew out a timeline to illustrate the effect of Christ's death on the cross.

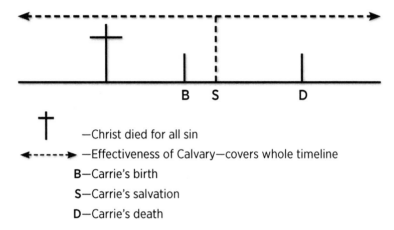

—Christ died for all sin

—Effectiveness of Calvary—covers whole timeline

B—Carrie's birth

S—Carrie's salvation

D—Carrie's death

"How many of your sins were future when Christ died?" I said.

"All of them—I hadn't been born yet."

"How many were paid for by Christ's death?"

"All," she whispered.

When we sin, we may feel distant from God, but he still loves us. He not only erases our sins, he forgets them (Isa. 43:25; Heb. 8:12). God does not deal with us the way a judge deals with a criminal. Our concerned Father grieves over our dangerous choices and their inevitable consequences. Biblical confession restores fellowship with God and peace in our hearts.

What Do I Confess?

We confess the truth: "I was wrong. I was naive. I betrayed myself by settling for less than I wanted. I ignored the warning signs of this disaster."[4]

We agree with God:

1. Father, you're right; I was wrong. I did it. I'm sorry.
2. Christ's sacrifice is sufficient. Thank you. Because of Jesus, I'm clean.

Carrie knelt and added the second part of confession. She left radiant. The next time I saw her, even her relationship with her husband had vastly improved. Receiving God's cleansing freed her to accept him. If God can do that for the sinner, we can be sure he'll grant healing and cleansing for the victims of sin, too.

Beauty from Ashes

One backlash from betrayal is a shaken identity. The searing event, murmurings, and surfacing hurt and anger cause us to wonder, *Who am I? I never used to feel so insecure.*

If Bathsheba had adopted the marred image put on her, I doubt she would have become David's respected queen or Solomon's wise teacher. The victim must confess God's view: *I am Christ's beloved. I have his righteousness.*

When someone betrays us, we use the idiom "I got burned." God uses the fire of betrayal to refine us. He burns away the chaff of an image that was built on others' opinions or our performance. In exchange, he gives us the beauty of a new identity based on Christ's righteousness.

What do you believe says more about who you are: this event or what Christ has done for you? Agree with God and experience the beauty of your Christian identity.

Why Do I Still Feel Guilty?

Many things make us feel soiled. Reading the sordid details of a crime in the newspaper can leave me wanting to wash my mind. Falling short of another's or my own expectations can make me feel condemned. Like sticky spider webs, invisible threads of regret and condemnation entangle us in self-absorption.

If you continue to experience condemnation after confessing your sins, agree with Romans 8:1: "There is now no condemnation for those who are in Christ Jesus."

How Does Correction Differ from Condemnation?

Don't confuse condemnation with the Holy Spirit's correction. Condemnation is usually a vague feeling that something is inherently wrong with me. God *never* condemns a believer. The world, the flesh, and the devil are the hurlers of these accusations (Rev. 12:10).

The Holy Spirit points out sin in order to free us from its grip. He identifies something specific to forsake: an action, attitude, or wrong belief. Whether you experience condemnation, conviction, or both, the solution is the same: agree with God's truth—about you and the situation.

Neither correction nor condemnation feels good, but "the sorrow that is according to the will of God produces a repentance without regret, leading to salvation; but the sorrow of the world produces death" (2 Cor. 7:10 NASB). God's correction produces positive change and eventual gratitude. Condemnation produces death—it's destructive and makes us cranky and self-absorbed. It doesn't move us closer to God.

The Holy Spirit always exalts Christ, not sin. The devil magnifies our failings and forecasts doom and gloom.

What If I Still Feel Dirty?

What do we do if we confess and forsake our sin, affirm our righteousness in Christ, but still feel dirty? We walk by faith, not by feelings. When we biblically confess our sins, by definition we're saying what God says: *Jesus took away all of my guilt and made me clean.* If we still feel guilty, we tell Satan out loud, "I belong to the Lord Jesus Christ and have his righteousness. Now leave."

Condemnation is spiritual warfare. Use your shield of faith to extinguish the enemy's fiery darts. Confess the truth of your standing in Christ (Eph. 6:16).

Let's Practice

1. Invite God to reveal any sin in your life (Ps. 139:23–24).

2. Write down what he shows you. This is not self-analysis. You've asked the Holy Spirit to search you. Biblical confession is Christ-centered, not me-centered. Sin can also be something we've failed to do. Ugly feelings that come from being exposed to sin can be acknowledged, too.

3. Write 1 John 1:9 out over your list. Thank him for his complete cleansing.

4. Finally, tear up your list to symbolize what God has done with your sins (Ps. 103:12).

God's power to cleanse is greater than sin's power to stain. The next time a snowflake wets your cheek, marvel: *God's made me as white as snow.*

I Want to Remember . . .

Today's takeaways from #LittleWomenBigGod are:

Prayer Requests

Record your small group's prayer requests here.

When You Yearn for Supernatural Strength

LET'S PLAY WORD ASSOCIATION. I'LL NAME AN ANIMAL, AND YOU name the trait you associate with it. For example, if I say "dove," you may say "innocent." What image do you associate with the following animals?

- Peacock –
- Fox –
- Snake –
- Lamb –

I bet you've heard people blame Bathsheba for David's fall. They're quick to point out how she bathed on her rooftop, and there is no record she resisted King David. But Nathan, speaking as God's prophet, portrays Bathsheba as a "little ewe lamb," slaughtered to satisfy David's visiting lust. What image does "little ewe lamb" convey?

The king had all power and authority. Even General Joab buckled under David's foolish demands (2 Sam. 24:3–4). History is filled with abusive authorities who preyed on those under their protection. Some lured their victims into traps. Others threatened them into compliance. A fish caught by biting a hook is no less prey than one speared. When a woman is drawn into a snare, she suffers self-condemnation for not recognizing the trap. Often these accusations are echoed by the culture, including friends and family.

Bathsheba bathed in the evening, perhaps under the cover of darkness, and when David should have been away at war. Her quarters were private and hidden from all eyes except those looking down from an elevated rooftop. If she tried to entice David, then she shares his blame. But Nathan's account mentions no seductive behavior on her part. She's the little lamb, and David is the powerful man who, according to David's own words, "deserves to die."

David's desires, not Bathsheba's, caused this tragedy. In a detailed word picture, Nathan describes a wealthy man, swollen with pride, who has no regard for his neighbor. He sent his men to seize this poor man's prized treasure. He used it and thought he could return it without the owner discovering the damage inflicted.

Only the treasure was a woman, the wife of one of his finest soldiers. Even if Bathsheba had not conceived, imagine how this shameful secret would have cut a wedge between her and Uriah, especially since Uriah worked for King David.

Bathsheba had no reason, that we know of, to mistrust David when he summoned her. Her family knew David. Her grandfather Ahithophel served David as a trusted counselor (2 Sam. 15:12). Her father and husband loyally served David on the battlefield. To misuse her would mean betraying them.

We know David tried to lower Uriah's defenses with gifts and drink. Had he done the same with Bathsheba? If Bathsheba felt lonely while her husband was away at war, alcohol could have made her more susceptible to the king's charms. Regardless of how we view this story, Nathan's clear account shows Bathsheba's trusted leader used her to satisfy his lust.

Bible stories are for our instruction (1 Cor. 10:11). If David, a man after God's own heart, could injure Bathsheba and so many others by his lack of self-control, what hope do you and I have? God has provided a way to escape our visiting lusts.

Day One
The Battle of Conflicting Desires

David's slide began before he noticed Bathsheba. While other kings were at war, David enjoyed his comfortable palace. Even though God had prohibited multiplying wives and concubines (Deut. 17:17), David collected women like some men collect fine wine (2 Sam. 5:13).

More is never enough for a discontented heart. To indulge our lusts feeds them instead of satisfying us. Let's look at the battle of conflicting desires.

Scripture Reading...

GALATIANS 5:16–26
So I say, walk by the Spirit, and you will not gratify the desires of the flesh. For the flesh desires what is contrary to the Spirit, and the Spirit what is contrary to the flesh. They are in conflict with

each other, so that you are not to do whatever you want. But if you are led by the Spirit, you are not under the law.

The acts of the flesh are obvious: sexual immorality, impurity and debauchery; idolatry and witchcraft; hatred, discord, jealousy, fits of rage, selfish ambition, dissensions, factions and envy; drunkenness, orgies, and the like. I warn you, as I did before, that those who live like this will not inherit the kingdom of God.

But the fruit of the Spirit is love, joy, peace, forbearance, kindness, goodness, faithfulness, gentleness and self-control. Against such things there is no law. Those who belong to Christ Jesus have crucified the flesh with its passions and desires. Since we live by the Spirit, let us keep in step with the Spirit. Let us not become conceited, provoking and envying each other.

Study and Reflection

1. Every Christian has a civil war inside. Who are the opposing sides in this battle?

2. What protects us from the sinful cravings of the flesh, also referred to as the "old nature" or "sinful nature" (Gal. 5:16)?

3. Review the acts of the flesh (Gal. 5:19–21). Circle the ones that relate to David and Bathsheba's story in 2 Samuel 11 and 12.

4. List the qualities the Holy Spirit produces in those who walk according to the Spirit (Gal. 5:22–23).

5. How does Ephesians 4:22 describe the desires that come from our old self? "You were taught, with regard to your former way of life, to put off your old self, which is being corrupted by its deceitful desires."

6. Why do you think the Scripture calls the desires generated by the flesh *deceitful*?

7. What other thoughts do you have about this passage?

The Battle Within

"Walk by the Spirit, and you will not gratify the desires of the flesh" (Gal. 5:16). Did you think your wrong desires would disappear when you came to Christ? Sadly, while we live in this world, we face an internal battle of conflicting desires. Our flesh continues to generate cravings that oppose God.

Bill Gillham defines the *flesh* as sin "impersonating the *old man* who was crucified with Christ . . . and that is why it seems like the old man is still alive."[1] Our old self was crucified with Christ, but sin still lives, and it masquerades as the old you. *Flesh* is also referred to as "indwelling sin" or the "sinful nature."

The Scripture calls the flesh's cravings "deceitful desires" because they lie to us. They promise happiness, but as David and Bathsheba illustrate, any pleasure is short-lived and soon turns into sorrow and regret (Heb. 11:25). These desires are also deceitful because they masquerade as *our* desires when they're really what our enemy wants for us.

New Covenant believers have two powerful assets David and Bathsheba lacked—a new identity and the indwelling Holy Spirit. "Therefore, if anyone is in Christ, the new creation has come: the old has gone, the new is here!" (2 Cor. 5:17). Sinful cravings may badger us, but we no longer have to obey them (Rom. 6:6–7). Nor do we want to. Since the new nature is patterned after Christ's, the true self loves, forgives, and wants to please God (Eph. 4:24). Every time we obey the flesh, we strengthen the influence of sin. Each Spirit-filled choice empowers our new nature.

In this context, the "flesh" does not refer to the physical body. Sinless Christ had human flesh. The flesh is our enemy, a parasite living within our physical bodies. Galatians 5 lists the obvious deeds of the flesh, but not every fleshly desire is visibly harmful. When I sit to read my Bible, a new catalogue may distract me. Before I know it, the time I had for Bible study is spent. My desire to read the catalogue wasn't inherently evil, but giving in to it during my Bible time robbed me.

People pleasers say yes to everyone, and workaholics won't say no to work. Both rob their families, souls, and God. Flesh is evil no matter how respectable it may appear.

I Want to Remember . . .

Write down any statements from today's lesson that will help you recall what God is teaching you. Let's encourage each other by sharing them on Twitter with the following hashtag: #LittleWomenBigGod

Today's takeaways from #LittleWomenBigGod are:

Day Two

Another Day, Another Battle

David obviously never considered how his actions would harm Bathsheba and countless others. Betrayal slices deeply into its victims. The wounded vacillate between brokenness, denial, and rage. Unbidden scenarios exposing and punishing the betrayer play through the victim's mind like a song stuck on repeat. Disoriented by dizzying emotions, the injured party may withdraw to gain her footing. What is real? Who can be trusted?

It is common to replay events and question our choices after we've been wronged. We berate ourselves for not recognizing the trap. We forget that only God is omniscient. All abuse breaks God's law of love. Sexual abuse is criminal, and the perpetrator is responsible. Yet victims search for something they could have done differently. They never want to go through so much pain again.

Victims don't cause the crimes against them. While discernment helps us avoid culpable people and compromising situations, for many there is no way to prevent the wrong. In Genesis, teenaged Joseph experienced gross unwarranted mistreatment from his ten older brothers. Later, as a slave, his master's wife lied about him. Joseph went to prison for doing the right thing. But God was with Joseph through all of these injustices.

Bathsheba could have blamed herself for Uriah's death. *Why didn't I tell him what had happened?* She could have withdrawn into shame or become promiscuous to affirm her marred image. Instead, her actions reveal someone who grieved her many losses and resisted the destructive thoughts and emotions that followed her pain.

If you've been a victim of any type of abuse, God knows the truth of what happened to you. He doesn't hold you responsible for sins committed against you. Resist the urge to withdraw, self-loath, or hate. Don't believe the lie that you deserved what happened or that you are now irreparably flawed. Your injury produces bitter thoughts like a wound produces infection. It must be cleansed with truth.

Use today's Scripture to overcome self-defeating thoughts. If you continue to struggle with condemnation, speak with a Christian counselor or mentor. You don't need to face this battle alone.

Scripture Reading...

2 Corinthians 10:3–5

For though we live in the world, we do not wage war as the world does. The weapons we fight with are not the weapons of the world. On the contrary, they have divine power to demolish strongholds. We demolish arguments and every pretension that sets itself up against the knowledge of God, and we take captive every thought to make it obedient to Christ.

Romans 8:6 NASB

For the mind set on the flesh is death, but the mind set on the Spirit is life and peace.

Romans 13:14

Rather, clothe yourselves with the Lord Jesus Christ, and do not think about how to gratify the desires of the flesh.

Study and Reflection

1. What types of struggles have you faced after you've been wronged?

2. Our minds become battlegrounds. Vengeful thoughts fight against the desire to forgive. Rage pounces on our peace. Self-reproach and self-pity wrestle against the longing to trust Christ. From today's Scripture, what role do our thoughts play in securing victory?

3. From 2 Corinthians 10:3–5, how do we fight the thoughts that argue against God's truth?

4. The following verse gives us something to do and something not to do. Practically speaking, how would you advise someone who is battling unhealthy inclinations? "Flee the evil desires of youth, and pursue righteousness, faith, love and peace, along with those who call on the Lord out of a pure heart" (2 Tim. 2:22).

5. What does God promise those who love his Word? "Great peace have those who love your law, and nothing can make them stumble" (Ps. 119:165).

6. What will we receive, *as we trust* in God? Relate this to battling defeating thoughts. "May the God of hope fill you with all joy and peace as you trust in him, so that you may overflow with hope by the power of the Holy Spirit" (Rom. 15:13).

Use Your Sword

The Word of God is called the sword of the Spirit (Eph. 6:17). Writing down Scripture that speaks to my vulnerable areas helps me. When I feel attacked, I open my journal and review God's precious words for me. Some carry their verses on index cards.

"Faith comes from hearing, and hearing by the word of Christ" (Rom. 10:17 NASB). "Pleasant words are . . . healing to the bones" (Prov. 16:24 NASB). When destructive thoughts attack your mind, take out your sWORD!

I Want to Remember . . .

Today's takeaways from #LittleWomenBigGod are:

Day Three
The Stakes Are High

God's cleansing does not eliminate the consequences of sin. Uriah was not resurrected. Sexually transmitted diseases don't disappear when we confess our sins. Loneliness and the pain of separation are natural results of breaking up a relationship, even a sinful one.

Even after we leave our sin, some unexpected repercussions continue. The consequences of seeds sown in sin live on. Some endure for a lifetime. David's sin affected his children. But these effects can make us wiser if we are walking with God. Living through sin's consequences helps us flee the next time temptation flirts.

Scripture Reading

2 Samuel 12:9–25

Study and Reflection

1. Nathan asked David why he had "*despised* the word of the Lord by doing evil." How does willful wrong show contempt for God? Relate this to David's actions.

2. List the consequences of David's sin.

3. What warning and hope do you get from the following? "Do not be deceived: God cannot be mocked. A man reaps what he sows. Whoever sows to please their flesh, from the flesh will reap destruction; whoever sows to please the Spirit, from the Spirit will reap eternal life. Let us not become weary in doing good, for at the proper time we will reap a harvest if we do not give up" (Gal. 6:7–9).

4. David was Bathsheba's trusted king and her husband's commander-in-chief. He was Israel's under-shepherd, the one who would write, "The Lord is my shepherd."

   a. What did Bathsheba lose because of David's sin against her?

   b. How would your relationship with this man be affected if you were in her shoes?

David Reaped What He'd Sown

Nathan's terrible predictions were fulfilled. David's oldest son Amnon, born to him by Ahinoam, raped his half-sister

Tamar. Tamar's brother, Absalom, avenged her by murdering Amnon. Absalom and Tamar were children of David and Maach. Absalom later attempted to wrench the kingdom from David. Ironically, in a pitched tent on David's rooftop, Absalom publicly took David's concubines in the way David had privately taken Uriah's wife (2 Sam. 16:21–22).

God cleansed and restored David after his sins against Bathsheba and Uriah, but David bore the earthly consequences. In Jeremiah 2:19, we read, "'Your wickedness will punish you; your backsliding will rebuke you. Consider then and realize how evil and bitter it is for you when you forsake the LORD your God and have no awe of me,' declares the Lord, the LORD Almighty.'"

God wipes away the sin that comes between him and us. He restores us to a place where we can be productive and thrive, but some of sin's consequences remain. Last week, we saw in a passage from James the great cost of sin. Now, we see our sin not only hurts us; it infects and injures those around us.

Are you involved in any activity or attitude that offends God? If so, seize this opportunity to confess and forsake it now. Avoid the inevitable heartache and harm that will come if you continue.

I Want to Remember . . .

Today's takeaways from #LittleWomenBigGod are:

Day Four
We Need a Helper

In the grocery store, my husband reminded me it's not a good idea to grocery shop while I'm hungry. One look in my cart and

I knew he was right. Functioning with a malnourished soul is like shopping when you're starved. Famished appetites overwhelm good sense.

The psalmist prayed, "Whom have I in heaven but You? And besides You, I desire nothing on earth" (Ps. 73:25 NASB). The closer I walk with Jesus, the less attractive wrong becomes.

Jesus, referring to the Holy Spirit's work in us, said rivers of living water will flow from us when we drink from him. Instead of being needy, we become a reservoir that refreshes others.

Lack of women was not David's problem. He had many wives and concubines. If he needed something, God would have given it (2 Sam. 12:8). The problem was internal, and so was the cure. Jesus said, "For out of the heart come evil thoughts—murder, adultery, sexual immorality, theft, false testimony, slander" (Matt. 15:19). Jim Cymbala says *since the problem is within us, Jesus sent the Holy Spirit to live inside of us.*

Romans 8:9 says every believer—not just those with special gifts and titles—has the Holy Spirit. In the Old Testament, the Holy Spirit anointed people for a mission or season and then left. Since Pentecost, the Spirit indwells every believer from the moment of spiritual birth. Our bodies are his home. We can grieve and suppress the Spirit, but he will never leave us. We're never alone in our battles. Embracing the ministry of the Holy Spirit will transform our lives.

Scripture Reading..

JOHN 7:37–39 NLT

On the last day, the climax of the festival, Jesus stood and shouted to the crowds, "Anyone who is thirsty may come to me! Anyone who believes in me may come and drink! For the Scriptures declare, 'Rivers of living water will flow from his heart.'" (When he said "living water," he was speaking of the Spirit, who would be given to everyone believing in him. But the Spirit had not yet been given, because Jesus had not yet entered into his glory.)

Study and Reflection

1. From today's Scripture, how can our thirsts benefit us?

2. What was Jesus referring to when he said, "Anyone who believes in me may come and drink" and "rivers of living water will flow from his heart"?

3. God's Spirit lives in us. Under each verse, write the practical benefits the Holy Spirit offers us. Personalize your answers.

   a. But the Advocate, the Holy Spirit, whom the Father will send in my name, will teach you all things and will remind you of everything I have said to you. (John 14:26)

   b. But when he, the Spirit of truth, comes, he will guide you into all the truth. He will not speak on his own; he will speak only what he hears, and he will tell you what is yet to come. He will glorify me because it is from me that he will receive what he will make known to you. (John 16:13–14)

   c. For you have not receive a spirit of slavery leading to fear again, but you have received a spirit of adoption as sons by which we cry out, "Abba! Father!" The Spirit Himself testifies with our spirit that we are children of God. (Rom. 8:15–16 NASB)

d. In the same way, the Spirit helps us in our weakness. We do not know what we ought to pray for, but the Spirit himself intercedes for us through wordless groans. And he who searches our hearts knows the mind of the Spirit, because the Spirit intercedes for God's people in accordance with the will of God. (Rom. 8:26–27)

e. What we have received is not the spirit of the world, but the Spirit who is from God, so that we may understand what God has freely given us. (1 Cor. 2:12)

f. For the Spirit God gave us does not make us timid, but gives us power, love and self-discipline. (2 Tim. 1:7)

4. How is relying on the Holy Spirit for strength different from exerting willpower? "For God is working in you, giving you the desire and the power to do what pleases him" (Phil. 2:13 NLT).

The Presence of God

Jesus told his disciples, "But very truly I tell you, it is for your good that I am going away. Unless I go away, the Advocate will not come to you; but if I go, I will send him to you" (John 16:7).

They must have scratched their heads. How could it be better for them for Jesus to be in heaven instead of with them on earth? How could any Advocate replace Jesus?

We know that this small band of believers would grow to cover the earth. While here, Jesus was limited to one place at a time. Now the Holy Spirit is with every child of God all the time. The Holy Spirit prays for us. That's right, he is praying for you right now! He reminds us we belong to God, leads us into all truth, comforts and counsels us. He is the one who gives us the ability to love God and resist sin. Having this Helper full time is indeed better.

A Christian's strength comes from trusting Christ. This is different from trying to restrain the flesh through self-effort. My friend Sandi's experience illustrates the difference focus makes. Growing up in New Orleans, Sandi rode bikes with her family on Sunday afternoons. Every week, her mom would say, "Sandi, don't hit the pedestrians." And every week, Sandi would run into one of them.

Sandi didn't want to hit the walkers. But when she was pedaling, she'd watch the people strolling next to her. Her bike followed her gaze. Sandi learned to ride safely among pedestrians when she learned to redirect her focus. How much better it is to practice God's presence than to focus on what we want to avoid. The closer we draw to Christ, the greater the family resemblance.

The Holy Spirit is our helper. Tomorrow we'll talk about how to be filled with him each day.

I Want to Remember . . .

Today's takeaways from #LittleWomenBigGod are:

Day Five
Appropriating Our Help

Intoxicated. What happens when people become intoxicated? If they are intoxicated with love, they are exhilarated. If they're intoxicated with alcohol, they're drunk. Intoxication changes people's speech, responses, and attitudes.

Ephesians 5:15–21 contrasts the difference between being controlled by alcoholic spirits and being filled with the Holy Spirit. What fills us controls us. Consider how different we act when we are filled with the following:

- Love versus hate
- Peace versus worry
- Joy versus sadness
- Hope versus despair
- Thankfulness versus grumbling
- Faithfulness versus flakiness

These contrasts reveal the difference between being filled with the Spirit and being controlled by the flesh. Today we look at how every believer can be filled with the Spirit and enjoy his life-changing power.

Scripture Reading....

EPHESIANS 5:15–21
Be very careful, then, how you live—not as unwise but as wise, making the most of every opportunity, because the days are evil. Therefore do not be foolish, but understand what the Lord's will is. Do not get drunk on wine, which leads to debauchery. Instead, be filled with the Spirit, speaking to one another with psalms, hymns, and songs from the Spirit. Sing and make music from your heart to the Lord, always giving thanks to God the Father for everything,

in the name of our Lord Jesus Christ. Submit to one another out of reverence for Christ.

Study and Reflection

1. In your own words, under each phrase, describe what a Spirit-filled life looks like.

    a. Communication with people: "Speaking to one another with psalms, hymns and songs from the Spirit."

    b. Communion with God: "Sing and make music from your heart to the Lord."

    c. Convictions about God and life: "Always giving thanks to God the Father for everything, in the name of our Lord Jesus Christ."

    d. Connections with others: "Submit to one another out of reverence for Christ."

2. Apply the following verses to your life.

    a. Do you not know that your bodies are temples of the Holy Spirit, who is in you, whom you have received from God? You are not your own. (1 Cor. 6:19)

b. And do not grieve the Holy Spirit of God, with whom you were sealed for the day of redemption. (Eph. 4:30)

3. The late Bill Bright, founder of Campus Crusade for Christ (Cru), used to say that living a life pleasing to God was not difficult; it was impossible. The only person able to live a life pleasing to God is Jesus Christ, and he wants to live it through us. From the verse below, what is our role in this relationship? "I have been crucified with Christ and I no longer live, but Christ lives in me. The life I now live in the body, I live by faith in the Son of God, who loved me and gave himself for me" (Gal. 2:20).

When You Yearn for Supernatural Strength . . . More Lessons from Bathsheba

Larry and I married at 4:00 P.M. on a blustery November afternoon in Savannah, Georgia. We pledged our love with heartfelt promises. Two hours later, we left for our honeymoon and had our first argument. What happened?

Sadly, good intentions—and even love—are not enough to check insecurity and selfishness. Today, we battle the same enemy David and Bathsheba faced—our flesh. Seminars and support groups promise techniques to manage our weaknesses:

- Anger management
- Addiction support
- Assertiveness training
- Communication techniques
- Marriage and parenting skills

While these may help, techniques alone can't provide the desire, motivation, or power to *be* a better person. We may be able to bite our tongues around the boss, but are we still seething inside? How do we break free from the limitations of our temperaments, family backgrounds, and insecurities?

Some believers, confused by ugly thoughts and desires, question their salvation. David loved God and yet sinned in a way that is hard to fathom. Bathsheba faced her own struggles. Let's look at the help God provides.

The Resources Within

God gave animals instincts. He gave humans himself. God created us to walk with him. If your Christian life has become boring or impotent, you may be missing out on the ministry of the Holy Spirit.

Every Christian has the Holy Spirit. We receive him the moment we come to Christ. "If anyone does not have the Spirit of Christ, they do not belong to Christ" (Rom. 8:9). But there is a difference between being indwelt by the Holy Spirit and being filled with him.

To illustrate the difference, picture making a glass of chocolate milk. When you add chocolate syrup to plain milk, the syrup settles in the bottom of the glass. The milk is *indwelt* with chocolate. If you took a sip before stirring it, you would taste plain milk. Stir the milk, and the syrup disperses throughout the glass. The milk is *filled* with chocolate. Now, every sip is chocolaty.

Christians can look and act like unbelievers even though we have the Holy Spirit. But when we are filled with the Spirit, we begin to look and taste like Christ! His love, joy, peace, patience, kindness, goodness, faithfulness, gentleness, and self-control disperse into every aspect of our lives (Gal. 5:22–23).

He's a Person, Not an It

The Holy Spirit is our personal helper, counselor, coach, comforter, and cheerleader. He knows the heart of our Father and is able to guide and empower us to live our best lives. Because he is a person, he wants and feels things. Our sin squashes his plans and hurts him.

Walking with God makes us more sensitive to sin. The sharp tongues we excused in the past now grieve the Holy Spirit within us. Our choices affect him. David felt the pain he'd caused God (Ps. 51:3–4).

Godly sorrow motivates constructive change. This is different from worldly guilt that shames us and makes us want to withdraw from God and those who walk with him (2 Cor. 7:10). Feeling the sorrow of our sin motivates us to forsake it.

The Holy Spirit is not some power we wield as we please. We don't live without a thought of God and then say, "Holy Spirit, fill me to witness to my neighbor." Rather, we surrender our total lives to him. We ask him to direct us in every area.

He's the hand that fills the glove. He's the mind and will that guides us. God does not divide our lives into sacred and secular. Everything is holy when done through him. This doesn't mean you will always sense his leading, but he directs the steps of those who ask. The late Donald Gray Barnhouse summed it up this way: *The Holy Spirit is not a power at our disposal to use as we wish, but a person who wants to possess our total being.*

The Role of Obedience

Romans 6:16 says we are slaves to the one we obey. We choose our master through obedience. Obeying sinful cravings puts our flesh in charge and desensitizes us to the Spirit's influence. Bowing to God releases his power to govern our will and emotions.

Surrendering to Christ's Lordship is synonymous with being filled with the Holy Spirit. We don't wait until our lives are sparkling clean to invite his filling. We ask him to help us forsake the things that grieve God, and he knows just what to do. But don't be surprised if he focuses on a different area of your life than the one that bothers you!

The Christian life is a walk of faith. Since we know God wants us to be filled with his Spirit, we can trust him to fill us when we ask. Faith, with or without an emotional experience, pleases God.

Are you ready to experience your best life (John 10:10)? Here is a suggested prayer to get you started:

> Dear Father,
> Thank you for your great love for me. Thank you for giving me your Holy Spirit. Please search me and point out any area that I need to confess and forsake. Thank you for your cleansing. Please fill me with your Holy Spirit. Take leadership over every area of my life: my thoughts, my will, my emotions, my words. Thank you for filling me. In Jesus' name. Amen.

Next week, we wrap up our study on Bathsheba by looking at the significant difference between biblical love, forgiveness, and trust. I can't wait for you to see how God turned Bathsheba's heartache into happiness.

I Want to Remember . . .

Today's takeaways from #LittleWomenBigGod are:

Prayer Requests

Record your small group's prayer requests here.

When You Hope to Move Forward

"Lust brought us together. We never should have married. I want a divorce."

My client thought her conclusion was airtight. Divorce was the only solution to a marriage founded on such a flimsy foundation. But she hadn't added God into her equation.

Many women have told me that even though they willingly participated in premarital sex with their husbands, they later felt used. They regretted their consent. They wished their husbands had led their dating relationship in sexual purity. Guilt's fangs now bit into their intimacy.

Thankfully, God is bigger than our failures and weaknesses. He took David and Bathsheba's marriage, which began with adultery, murder, and an unwed pregnancy, and turned it into a partnership of mutual love and respect that produced kings in the lineage of Christ. He wants to redeem our bad starts, too.

You may wonder why we're spending another week on Bathsheba. Bathsheba's challenges relate, in some degree, to all of us. Who hasn't had to forgive? Who hasn't battled self-defeating thoughts? I couldn't skip the essential life skills Bathsheba's drama offers. They help us know how to move from victim to superconqueror in our own challenges.

David and Bathsheba show that marriages with poor beginnings can succeed. As both partners grow, forgive, and show preference for one another, the relationship transforms to reflect the individuals' improved characters. Change begins with repentance—a change of heart that leads to change of behavior. If the heart doesn't change, then new behavior will be short-lived. David's cold heart had Uriah carry the letter that bore his own death sentence. David's renewed heart led him to fast and pray for the life of his infant and write psalms to the Lord. Bathsheba witnessed David's genuine brokenness and opened her heart to him.

God blessed their union with four sons. Solomon became Israel's grandest and wisest king. He built God's temple and wrote Song of Solomon, Ecclesiastes, and much of Proverbs. Jesus received his right to the throne through Solomon's bloodline. Mary, the mother of Jesus, was a descendant of Nathan, another of David and Bathsheba's sons.

God turned Bathsheba and David's bad beginning into a glorious ending. Maybe you had a poor start in life, in parenting, or in personal development. Imagine how God might turn your inadequate beginning into a fabulous ending if you'll trust him.

Love Biblically

Loss touches even the animal kingdom. After a Doberman gave birth to six puppies, one died. When the owner "showed the mother the deceased pup, she lovingly tried to kiss it back to life. When she realized the pup was dead, she ultimately began to grieve and weep."[1]

Bathsheba felt her losses, too. Nathan's account shows a close relationship between her and Uriah. Imagine grieving the loss of your husband while married to the one responsible for his death. On the heels of this trauma came the sickness and death of her firstborn (2 Sam. 12:15–24). But there is a light in this dark passage. David's heart has changed. His response to Nathan and his son's illness reveals a genuine return to the Lord.

Mending a broken relationship is daunting. We worry, *Will I get hurt again? Can I trust this person?* This week, we'll consider four aspects of restoration—love, forgiveness, reconciliation, and trust.[2]

If your soul has been rubbed raw by a painful relationship, you may want to resist these teachings. Please don't. Ask God to open your heart to hear his perspective on your individual circumstance. God's ways are for your best.

Reconciliation takes two people. Some relationships won't be healed. But when we do our part, we experience peace of mind, inner healing, and God's comfort. Today we begin with biblical love.

Scripture Reading...
2 SAMUEL 12:15–25

Study and Reflection

1. Bathsheba, being one of many wives, certainly had different expectations for her marriage than we have for our husbands. Yet she was a woman with real emotions. Do you think David's actions while their son was dying comforted or irritated Bathsheba? Why?

2. Bathsheba allowed David to comfort her (2 Sam. 12:24–25). What do you think that says about her attitude toward David?

3. In the following verses, who benefits when we show love?

   a. The merciful man does himself good, but the cruel man does himself harm. (Prov. 11:17 NASB)

   b. "And the King will say, 'I tell you the truth, when you did it to one of the least of these my brothers and sisters, you were doing it to me!'" (Matt. 25:40 NLT)

   c. But love your enemies, do good to them, and lend to them without expecting to get anything back. Then your reward will be great, and you will be children of the Most High, because he is kind to the ungrateful and wicked. (Luke 6:35)

4. The Bible commands us to love everyone, *even our enemies.* From the verses that follow, why should we continue to love

even when we're hurt? "Let no debt remain outstanding, except the continuing debt to love one another, for whoever loves others has fulfilled the law. The commandments, 'You shall not commit adultery,' 'You shall not murder,' 'You shall not steal,' 'You shall not covet,' and whatever other command there may be, are summed up in this one command: 'Love your neighbor as yourself.' Love does no harm to a neighbor. Therefore love is the fulfillment of the law" (Rom. 13:8–10).

5. Before David married Bathsheba, he behaved like her enemy. Apply the following verses to loving someone who has wronged you.

   a. But I tell you, love your enemies and pray for those who persecute you, that you may be children of your Father in heaven. He causes his sun to rise on the evil and the good, and sends rain on the righteous and the unrighteous. If you love those who love you, what reward will you get? Are not even the tax collectors doing that? And if you greet only your own people, what are you doing more than others? Do not even pagans do that? Be perfect, therefore, as your heavenly Father is perfect. (Matt. 5:44–48)

   b. "But to you who are listening I say: Love your enemies, do good to those who hate you, bless those who curse you, pray for those who mistreat you. . . . Be merciful, just as your Father is merciful." (Luke 6:27–28, 36)

 c. But God demonstrates His own love toward us, in that while we were yet sinners, Christ died for us. . . . For if while we were enemies we were reconciled to God through the death of His Son, much more, having been reconciled, we shall be saved by His life. (Rom. 5:8, 10 NASB)

 d. Love is patient, love is kind. It does not envy, it does not boast, it is not proud. It does not dishonor others, it is not self-seeking, it is not easily angered, it keeps no record of wrongs. (1 Cor. 13:4–5)

6. Why is loving someone not the same as tolerating or accepting their wrong actions? "Love must be sincere. Hate what is evil; cling to what is good" (Rom. 12:9).

Biblical Love Is Tough Love

One of the unexpected fallouts of betrayal is that people treat you differently. In a divorce caused by infidelity, family members and friends don't know how to act around the faithful spouse. Some feel awkward and withdraw. Others assign shared blame. They don't want to wrestle with their confusion.

David was the king. How could his servants and friends protect their ease in relating to him if he's a villain? It would be easier to blame Bathsheba and make David the victim. That way, their world's protected.

After we've been burned, our ability to love takes a hit. Love based on how other people treat us or on how deserving they are will turn to ashes. But God has a better idea. From the ashes of burned-up conditional love, the phoenix of unconditional love rises. Biblical love is strong and resilient because it comes from God instead of from fickle emotions. Unconditional love is as steady as the character of the lover. It is not based on the worthiness of the recipient.

Genuine love is tough and able to maintain protective boundaries. It is displayed through actions. The greatest demonstration of love took place on the cross, while we were God's enemies (Rom. 5:10). Love seeks the eternal best for its object. It fulfills all of God's laws. When God says to love our enemies, he isn't asking us to manufacture a warm glow. He calls us to do the right thing.

God told the Israelites to return their brother's stray ox or donkey when they found it (Deut. 22:1). If they found their enemy's lost animal, they were to return it, too (Exod. 23:4). In other words, do the right thing whether the other person deserves it or not—you deserve it.

Research shows that we can't focus on two opposite emotions for the same person at the same time.[3] Being good to everyone shows we belong to God and prospers *our* souls.

Biblical Love Is Not Tolerance

The instruction to love our enemies does not mean to tolerate sin or abuse. Permitting sin is not good for us or them. Love and boundaries go together.

When the first man, Adam, rebelled against God, God removed him from Eden. This protected Adam from eating from the Tree of Life and being sealed into his sinful state. Love motivates us to set limits on what we allow in relationships. Enabling someone to continue in wrong is not love. Love says, "Allowing you to rage at me is not good for either of us. I'm going to my bedroom. When you have calmed down, I'll hear your thoughts." Self-control and love come from the Spirit.

David hid from King Saul to keep from being killed. Yet when given the opportunity, he refused to retaliate or curse Saul.

Jesus demonstrated the firm and soft sides of love. He blasted the Pharisees for their hypocrisy and refused to speak to Herod, who had beheaded John the Baptist (Luke 23:9). Yet he wept over Jerusalem and went to the cross for all of these people (Matt. 23:37). As C. S. Lewis said in *The Problem of Pain,* "Love is something more stern and splendid than mere kindness."[4]

God's command to love everyone sounds crazy in some contexts. But God cares about *our* character. He wants us to be loving people. After all, we live with ourselves. Don't allow someone else's sin to embitter you.

Who is the last person on earth you want to love? This is your "least of these." As we treat them, so we treat him.[5] When you show kindness to that person, remember you do it for Jesus. Ask our big God to fill you with his Holy Spirit and love through you. Remember, since God *is* love, he is able to love others through his surrendered child (John 13:35; 1 John 4:15–21).

God uses the challenge of difficult people to burn away the chaff of conditional love and give us the beauty of unconditional love. We no longer love people because of what they do for us. We love them because God loves us and loves through us. The next time someone burns you, remember: God brings beauty from ashes.

I Want to Remember . . .

Write down any statements from today's lesson that will help you recall what God is teaching you. Let's encourage each other by sharing them on Twitter with the following hashtag: #LittleWomenBigGod

Today's takeaways from #LittleWomenBigGod are:

Forgive for Your Sake

"Forgive her? No need. It's no big deal."

Or, "Forgive her? No way! What she did was too terrible to forgive."

Brushing an offense off may be an avoidance tactic. Saying something is too big to forgive keeps us in bondage. Bathsheba had some serious injuries to forgive, but small offenses can also bother us. Big or small, God's way to deal with injuries is to forgive.

In today's passage, the king represents God. The slave who owed the king the equivalent of our national debt represents you and me. Ask God to give you fresh insight into today's passage.

Scripture Reading...

MATTHEW 18:21–35
Then Peter came to Jesus and asked, "Lord, how many times shall I forgive my brother or sister who sins against me? Up to seven times?"

Jesus answered, "I tell you, not seven times, but seventy-seven times.

"Therefore, the kingdom of heaven is like a king who wanted to settle accounts with his servants. As he began the settlement, a man who owed him ten thousand bags of gold was brought to him. Since he was not able to pay, the master ordered that he and his wife and his children and all that he had be sold to repay the debt.

"At this the servant fell on his knees before him. 'Be patient with me,' he begged, 'and I will pay back everything.' The servant's master took pity on him, canceled the debt and let him go.

"But when that servant went out, he found one of his fellow servants who owed him a hundred silver coins. He grabbed him and began to choke him. 'Pay back what you owe me!' he demanded.

"His fellow servant fell to his knees and begged him, 'Be patient with me, and I will pay it back.'

"But he refused. Instead, he went off and had the man thrown into prison until he could pay the debt. When the other servants saw what had happened, they were outraged and went and told their master everything that had happened.

"Then the master called the servant in. 'You wicked servant,' he said, 'I canceled all that debt of yours because you begged me to. Shouldn't you have had mercy on your fellow servant just as I had on you?' In anger his master handed him over to the jailers to be tortured, until he should pay back all he owed.

"This is how my heavenly Father will treat each of you unless you forgive your brother or sister from your heart."

Study and Reflection

1. From the following, whom should we forgive? "And forgive us our sins, as we have forgiven those who sin against us" (Matt. 6:12 NLT).

2. How often and why do we forgive (Matt. 18:21–35)?

3. What would have happened to the slave if the king had not
    forgiven him (Matt. 18:25)?

4. What would have happened to us if God had not shown us
    compassion? "For God so loved the world that he gave his
    one and only Son, that whoever believes in him shall not
    perish but have eternal life" (John 3:16).

5. The servant couldn't have repaid the debt if he had ten life-
    times. The king understood this and forgave the debt. What
    did forgiving cost the king?

6. After the king saved the servant and his family from prison,
    how would you expect this freed man to treat others (verses
    32–33)?

7. Why do you think he hunted down the one who owed him
    so little by comparison?

8. Who was affected by this slave's unforgiving actions (Matt.
    18:31)?

9. What does the king call the forgiven slave who refused to
    forgive?

10. Perhaps "torturers" (verses 34–35) refers to bitter feelings. How does bitterness torment us?

It's Not Fair

There are many reasons forgiveness seems unfair. Doesn't justice demand that a wrongdoer pay for her crime?

Forgiving doesn't undo a wrong. Forgiving the drunk driver who crippled you won't restore your legs. People who injure us can't rewind time and undo the harm they've caused. We have to live with the consequences of their sin. When the king in today's story canceled the slave's debt, no one restored his royal bank account. He had to live without the money owed him.

It is easy to focus on wrongs committed against us and forget the debt we owe Christ. Nathan reminded David our wrongs against each other are sins against God.

The king in Matthew's story represents Christ. It would have been fair for him to leave us in Satan's clutches. Instead, he paid our debt with his own blood. The slave who was forgiven represents us. We owe Jesus a debt we can never pay.

Maybe you've wondered what you did that could equal the horrible wrongs committed against you. Like David, our sins brought death. They sent God's only Son to the cross.

You and I will never go to hell because of someone's sin against us. But Jesus suffered hell on the cross for our wrongs. And he did this while we were his enemies (Rom. 5:8–10). He also suffered for every offense committed against us. If we hold someone's sin against him or her, we become like the wicked servant. We tell Jesus his suffering was not enough.

The next time you need to forgive someone, remember how much you've been forgiven. It would be unfair to Jesus—and to ourselves—not to forgive.

It Hurts

I grew up watching TV Westerns. It made me wince to watch someone cut a lodged arrow out of a wounded cowboy. For some reason, releasing a wrong often feels like removing a barbed arrow out of bleeding flesh. To forgive we must *let go* of the offense.

The benefit of letting go is health. The relief is similar to how one feels after vomiting up toxins. I hate to throw up. But I love the relief that comes afterwards.

I've sat with many women as, one by one, they forgave horrendous wrongs, including repeated incest and gang rape. The process was wrenching, but their tears gave way to relief. And they no longer feared poisoning their loved ones with bitterness (Matt. 18:32–35; Heb. 12:15). The temporary pain of forgiving can't compare with the everlasting torment of living with bitterness. It hurts more *not* to forgive.

I Can't Let Go

In tug-of-war, two people hold opposite ends of a rope. When one person pulls the rope, the other is jerked. Bitterness ties us to the one who wronged us. Every time we see the offender, or remember how she hurt us, our wound is tugged. When we forgive, we drop our end of the rope.

The other person may continue to jerk the rope, but if we've let go, his actions no longer control us. When we forgive, we quit trying to collect the love, respect, or apologies the offender owes us. When we believe our King has canceled our debt and bountifully supplied our every need, we're no longer compelled to collect wooden nickels from slaves.

Deep hurts take time to heal. Don't confuse pain with bitterness. This week's closing addresses this. The culprit may not acknowledge their wrong or appreciate our forgiveness. But Jesus receives our forgiveness as a beautiful gift (Matt. 25:40).

How to Forgive, through the Power of the Holy Spirit

1. Acknowledge the offense to God. Look at this as documenting the wrong.
2. Include how you felt. "I forgive my mother for preferring my older brother even though I felt worthless and unloved." Hand over each hurt to God until you have nothing more to forgive that person.
3. Commit the offender and the offense to God. In a sense, you are turning him or her over to a collection agency named *God*. That means you have given up the right to punish, seek revenge, and force them to agree with your point of view. You won't continue to be tied to them by trying to collect apologies or acknowledgments of their wrong.
4. Ask God to deal with the offender in the appropriate way by causing his best for all involved: *Lord, I commit this person and this offense into your hands. I trust you to work this for my good and the good of all who love you. Please, work in this person's life for his or her eternal good.*

If you have many people to forgive, forgive each one individually. If the pain continues or returns, affirm your decision to turn the offender and the offense over to God. Thank him that he's taken it and will use it for the eternal good of all who love him (Rom. 8:28–29).

I Can't Confront Them

Forgiveness is between God and us. We don't have to contact the one we're forgiving. She may be dead. He may deny it, blame us, or minimize what he did and wound us more.

A woman said that hearing she didn't have to confront her father to forgive him freed her. He'd sexually abused her sister and her while they were growing up. She lived trapped in bitterness because she knew she could never approach him on this.

"When you said forgiveness was between me and God, and I did not have to address the person who wronged me, I knew I wanted to forgive my father." She forgave every long-harbored hurt. Later that week her father called her. "For the first time in my adult life, I was able to talk with him without knots in my stomach." She was free!

Forgive for your sake. Forgive for Christ's sake. Bathsheba did. Her life shows the reward that came from forgiveness.

Whew, we've covered some heavy topics. You now know more than most about real love and forgiveness. Tomorrow we explore the secrets of *reconciliation* and *trust*. I think you'll enjoy this.

I Want to Remember . . .

Today's takeaways from #LittleWomenBigGod are:

Day Three
Restore Trust—Carefully

Bathsheba suffered much following the dark night David summoned her. She may have wondered what kind of future her marriage held for her.

Shattered trust must be rebuilt for a partnership to flourish. If a new relationship starts at zero, after betrayal a relationship is at a minus. Bathsheba's trust of David must have been at a negative one hundred.

It takes time to restore faith. Trust is earned, not instant. Don't beat yourself up when your feelings don't immediately bounce back after a breech in fidelity.

Trust will suffer as long as either party continues in willful sin. David built trust with Bathsheba by owning his sin, restoring his relationship with God, and returning to righteous living.

After the prophet Nathan confronted David over his sin concerning Bathsheba and Uriah, David wrote Psalm 51. The superscription says it is for the choir director. This indicates it was used in public worship. As you read this psalm, think of the context in which David penned it.

Scripture Reading...

Psalm 51:1–13

Study and Reflection

1. How could this public confession have helped Bathsheba's opinion of David?

2. What does David's psalm reveal about his character and relationship with God?

3. How does he view God's judgment (verse 4)?

4. When reestablishing trust, how important is it for the offender not only to be sorry for hurting the victim but also be broken before God?

5. What do you learn from the following, and how could this have helped restore Bathsheba's trust in David? "For David

had done what was right in the eyes of the LORD and had not failed to keep any of the LORD's commands all the days of his life—except in the case of Uriah the Hittite" (1 Kings 15:5).

6. The Bible never tells us to trust everyone. What warnings do you receive from the following verses?

   a. Walk with the wise and become wise, for a companion of fools suffers harm. (Prov. 13:20)

   b. Do not make friends with a hot-tempered person, do not associate with one easily angered, or you may learn their ways and get yourself ensnared. (Prov. 22:24–25)

   c. Do not speak to fools, for they will scorn your prudent words. (Prov. 23:9)

   d. Do not be misled: "Bad company corrupts good character." (1 Cor. 15:33)

7. Some people feel bad about themselves when they don't trust someone. Trust, like faith, is only as good as its object. God doesn't tell us to trust people indiscriminately. What do you learn from the following verses on trust?

   a. Now while he was in Jerusalem at the Passover Festival, many people saw the signs he was performing and believed in his name. But Jesus would not entrust himself to them, for he knew all people. He did not need any testimony about mankind, for he knew what was in each person. (John 2:23–25)

b. When they hurled their insults at him, he did not retaliate; when he suffered, he made no threats. Instead, he entrusted himself to him who judges justly. (1 Pet. 2:23)

8. When we're unsure about a relationship, we walk by faith and practice the light God has provided in his Word. Apply the following promise to those who are seeking to follow God in a difficult relationship. "And we know that in all things God works for the good of those who love him, who have been called according to his purpose" (Rom. 8:28).

Proceed Wisely

The Scripture says, "If it is possible, as far as it depends on you, live at peace with everyone" (Rom. 12:18). It's not possible to live at peace with everyone. But this verse reminds us the lack of relationship should be because of the other person's sin, not our stubbornness. Jesus could not live at peace with the hypocritical Pharisees and still be in sync with his Father. How can I, and my household, serve the Lord and tolerate sin at the same time (Josh. 24:15)?

There is an important difference between forgiveness and reconciliation. We don't have to involve the offender to forgive him or her. But reconciliation requires the cooperation of both people. Conversations may be necessary to work through the hurt. Our part is to forgive and speak the truth in love (Eph. 4:15, 25). We are not responsible for the other person's words or attitudes. But we are responsible for ourselves.

If you feel led to approach the person who injured you, first make sure your heart is clean. Vent your hurt feelings in a journal or letter to God. Let go of the wrong and allow God to comfort you. Receive his perspective. Indiscriminately dumping hurt and anger does not clear the air or help someone hear us. Sometimes after we forgive, we no longer feel the need to approach the offender.

Our aim should be to win the person back, not to punish them (Matt. 18:15). We bring up an offense to clarify a misunderstanding or to provide an opportunity for repentance. Vengeance belongs to God (Rom. 12:19).

We can't change an offender into a safe person. We can appeal to him or her, but we cannot make someone understand our viewpoint or want a healthy relationship with us. Jesus longed to gather Israel under his wings as a mother hen does her baby chicks, but they were unwilling (Matt. 23:37). People who welcome honest conversation without undue defensiveness have the potential to build healthy relationships. Those who blame others for their failings are poor candidates for safe relationships.

Well-meaning people may tell us how it will honor God if we reconcile with the offender. However, if the person is unrepentant, trying to reconcile may be foolish.

It Takes Two

Broken relationships can heal. Trust can be restored, but only when both people want to walk together in righteousness. "What fellowship can light have with darkness?" (2 Cor. 6:14). The relationship won't heal while either clings to sin or bitterness.

But God uses even this for the good of those who love him. He uses the affliction of betrayal and broken relationships to burn out the chaff in our character and replace it with the beauty of his character. He makes us beautiful through the process.

I Want to Remember . . .

Today's takeaways from #LittleWomenBigGod are:

Day Four
Moving Forward

Of David's numerous sons from his many wives, God chose two of Bathsheba's sons to be in Jesus' genealogy! Bathsheba overcame her losses and blessed the generations that followed.

Scripture Reading...

1 CHRONICLES 3:1–9

PROVERBS 31:1–5

Study and Reflection

1. From which of David's sons does Mary, Jesus' mother, come? ". . . the son of Melea, the son of Menna, the son of Mattatha, the son of Nathan, the son of David" (Luke 3:31).

2. To which of David's sons does this verse trace the kingly line of Joseph, Jesus' adopted father? ". . . Jesse the father of King

David. David was the father of Solomon, whose mother had been Uriah's wife" (Matt. 1:6).

3. David and Bathsheba named one of their sons Nathan, the name of the prophet who confronted David about his sin. From the verses that follow, what does this tell you about David and Bathsheba?

   a. Do not rebuke mockers or they will hate you; rebuke the wise and they will love you. (Prov. 9:8)

   b. Whoever rebukes a person will in the end gain favor rather than one who has a flattering tongue. (Prov. 28:23)

4. *The Ryrie Study Bible* says King Lemuel, in Proverbs 31, may have been King Solomon. Lemuel means "belonging to God" and could have been Bathsheba's special name for her son.[6] Knowing Bathsheba's history, read Proverbs 31:1–5. What phrases in this mother's wisdom to her royal son could have been learned from her early experience with King David?

Wisdom's Warning

I have counseled many women whose experiences with inappropriate sex were linked to alcohol. Alcohol lowered their resolve or their defenses and made them vulnerable to compromise or abuse. Suddenly, an innocent back rub turned into betrayal and tears.

David "made [Uriah] drunk" in his attempt to manipulate him (2 Sam. 11:13). He may have done the same to Bathsheba. Proverbs 31 says drink clouds judgment and causes kings to pervert the rights of the oppressed. Perhaps David was drinking when he summoned Bathsheba and sent Uriah to his death.

Learn from the wisdom of Proverbs. Princesses also need to beware of strong drink and men who crave it.

I Want to Remember . . .

Today's takeaways from #LittleWomenBigGod are:

Day Five
Enjoy God's Awesome Handiwork

Sometime in their lives, David promised Bathsheba that her son would inherit the throne (1 Kings 1:13, 17, 30; 1 Chron. 22:9–10). David had sons from other wives and concubines before he married Bathsheba, so this was a great promise to her. Perhaps this was one of the ways David comforted Bathsheba after the death of their firstborn. Solomon was God's gift after that loss.

King David was seventy years old when the plot to steal the throne took place (2 Sam. 5:4). He and Bathsheba had been together about twenty years.

Because David's worn body could not keep warm, a young virgin was chosen to be his nurse and lie close to him to keep him warm. Even though David never had sexual relations with Abishag, she was considered one of his concubines. Adonijah was Solomon's older brother by a different mother. Ryrie calls Adonijah's request for Abishag "a scheme to gain the throne" from Solomon.[7]

After Solomon's crowning, Bathsheba became the queen mother. Was she naive or politically astute when she relayed Adonijah's request to Solomon? A desire to restore harmony in the family may have dulled her powers of discernment. Or did she agree to relay his request because she knew wise Solomon would see the threat Adonijah posed?

Scripture Reading...

1 KINGS 1

1 KINGS 2:12–25

Study and Reflection

1. What role did Bathsheba play in securing the throne for Solomon? What was at stake for her and Solomon if Adonijah became king?

2. Why do you think Nathan needed Bathsheba to participate in the plan to seat Solomon as king?

3. Notice how King Solomon greeted Bathsheba (1 Kings 2:19). What does that tell you about their relationship?

4. How did Solomon respond to Bathsheba's message?

5. In what ways do you identify with or admire Bathsheba?

6. What did you learn about God from Bathsheba's story?

7. What do you want to remember from Bathsheba?

When You Hope to Move Forward . . . Additional Lessons from Bathsheba

After watching Bathsheba bathe, King David needed a bath. If David had taken his lustful desires to God, God would have cleansed him. David would have avoided years of tragedy, heartbreak, and loss. Instead, his thoughts took action. Many innocent people were sacrificed on the altar of David's desires, including Israel's soldiers who fought beside Uriah when David had him killed.

David's sin infected his family. Just as Nathan had predicted, the sword that hurt David most came from within his own household (2 Sam. 12:10–19). Sin is a crooked path. We can never predict where it will lead. Referring to this part of David's life, someone said, "Sin will take you farther than you ever wanted to go, cost you more than you ever wanted to pay, and keep you longer than you ever wanted to stay."

Some see sin's consequences as an expression of God's anger. While God disciplines those he loves, he goes to great trouble to warn against sin's inevitable outcome. Many consequences are built into sin. When you put your hand on a hot burner, someone doesn't come and blister your hand to teach you a lesson. The blisters are a natural result. So it is when we depart from God's clear path; sin affects us—and those we love.

A woman whose husband abandoned her for another woman asked me, "What did I do to deserve this?"

Her husband had cheated on her before marriage, but because she was already sexually connected to him, she married him anyway. If she had been committed to purity, she would not have married him. Could the choices she made long ago be a factor to today's pain? I think so.

Driving down the wrong side of the highway is hazardous. But tragically, even when we are on the right side of the road, we can still be injured. Someone, carelessly or defiantly, can cross into our lane.

Nathan describes Uriah and Bathsheba as such victims. For many, her reputation is linked to this sordid event. Parents name their sons David, but how many girls do you know named Bathsheba?

Forgiveness Brings Rewards

To forgive and live with David after so much pain seems impossible. Yet Bathsheba forgave David. She chose to trust God with her reputation, her losses, and her life. God rewarded her with influence in the lives of Israel's two greatest kings. Two of her sons are part of Jesus' genealogy. No other woman holds that distinction.

Israel's wisest king, Solomon, is the ancestor of Joseph, Jesus' adopted father. Through this line, Jesus received his right to be king. Through his mother, Mary, Jesus was the descendant of Bathsheba's son Nathan.

God cursed the kingly line of David in later generations for their wickedness. Rabbis scratched their heads, trying to understand how the Messiah could inherit David's throne and not be of the cursed royal bloodline. The solution: the Messiah would be born of a virgin from the nonroyal bloodline of David and receive the royal title from his adopted father. Both lines came from David and Bathsheba.

Some portray Bathsheba as a seductress. That doesn't fit the Scripture's description. Bathsheba was bathing in her private quarters at night. David could have turned away when he saw her. He could have decided not to inquire about her. When he learned she was married, he did not have to send messengers to take her. We wouldn't send someone to seize a beautiful trinket we saw in someone's house.

David did not have to violate her. After her pregnancy threatened to expose his sin, he could have confessed. Instead, he plunged deeper and deeper into deception, sending Uriah to his death. Sin took David farther than he planned to go.

Perhaps Bathsheba was naive. Maybe David's wine, charm, and royal authority seduced her. Maybe she should have found another place to bathe. But based on Nathan's description depicting her as a "little ewe lamb," God clearly held David responsible.

Many victims who have suffered sexual abuse at a young age blame themselves for not stopping the abuse. This blame is mislaid. Such victims should receive comfort from God's judgment in this story. The abuser, not the victim, was held responsible. David was "the man" who deserved death. And David's sons from other marriages fulfilled God's judgment spoken by Nathan.

Our culture places a high value on sex appeal. Bathsheba's beauty made her prey to David's lust. This was not her fault. If she had intentionally allured him with her beauty, that would have been her sin. It is not unusual for abusers and society to blame the woman for the abuse. The abuser may tell his victim the abuse is her fault. He may even call it "love." When the sexual abuser is someone trusted, this is especially confusing.

After abuse, the victim feels damaged and branded. Satan delights in such a response. While Bathsheba may have felt these emotions, she overcame them to become an influential queen. Perhaps her ears were the first to hear David strum his harp and sing his new psalms. She believed if God had cleansed David, surely he had washed away her victim's stain as well.

Moving Forward

Psalm 51 was presented to the choir director after Nathan confronted David over his sin. In other words, David publicly accepted full responsibility for his actions. He did not blame Bathsheba but sought to restore her faith in him.

David's psalms demonstrated his return to God. Nothing reassures a woman of faith more than to see her man rightly connected with God. If David had owned his sin with Bathsheba, but not with God, I doubt she would have fully trusted him.

If ever a marriage had a bad start, this one did. Besides being used as an object, having her reputation tarnished, and the loss of her husband Uriah, she lost her first child. Losing a child puts an enormous stress on a couple. Instead of blaming David for her many losses, Bathsheba welcomed his comfort. Her willingness to weed out the seed of bitterness before it took root is a testimony to her own relationship with God.

If Bathsheba had held on to her pain and shame and withdrawn from David and the royal court, what blessings she (and we) would have missed. Some believe Proverbs 31 records the lessons Solomon learned from Bathsheba. Her influence helped secure the throne for Solomon. This queen reveals the blessings that come to those who receive God's healing and extend forgiveness.

Cleaning the Wound

Biblical forgiveness is an essential life skill. Forgiving a wrong cleanses an emotional wound so we'll heal without infection.

Physical wounds help us understand emotional wounds. Without cleaning, infection can set in and spread. Washing a surface scratch won't sting, but just blowing on a deep wound will cause a wince. The deeper the wound, the more tender it is to touch. Deeper wounds need cleaning more often than scratches. A deep injury oozes after cleansing and must be repeatedly bathed and dressed. The frequency of tending the wound decreases with healing.

The deeper the injury, the more painful the act of forgiving. Some wrongs are easily forgiven. Others, like oozing wounds, continue to seep pain. Don't beat up on yourself if this happens. Just "clean" your wound again. Reaffirm your forgiveness. As you heal, those times will occur less often.

A deep wound may throb when knocked, even after it appears to be healed—even years later. Reminders from the past, or a chance meeting with someone associated with an injury may ding an emotional injury. This throbbing may hurt deeply but usually won't last long.

We can't heal our wounds, but we can support the healing process with good nutrition and hygiene. Wounds heal in a healthy body. Our bodies heal different wounds at varying rates. Some heal quickly and never bother us again. Others act up under stress or weather changes. Some leave scars to remind us of our battles.

We clean our wounds as often as the wound seeps bitter thoughts and emotions. We nourish our spiritual life with his Word and by fellowshipping with God and his body, the church (Eph. 5:26). "Then they cried to the LORD in their trouble, and he saved them from their distress. He sent out his word and healed them" (Ps. 107:19–20).

Are you experiencing a fresh wound? What old wound has recently been knocked? Wash your wound and forgive (again) the person who hurt you. Nurture yourself with God's Word and trusted godly friends. Be reconciled with those who sincerely turn away from evil.

Bathsheba refused to receive the branding of the world. So can we. By forgiving ourselves and extending grace and forgiveness to those who've hurt us, we receive freedom from the past. A forgiving life is a free life. God is greater than our injuries. He granted grace to Bathsheba and David and will do so for you.

I Want to Remember . . .

Today's takeaways from #LittleWomenBigGod are:

Prayer Requests

Record your small group's prayer requests here.

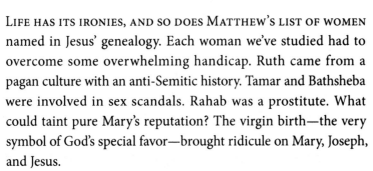

When You Face the Impossible

Mary means "their rebellion."

What a fool I've been. Joseph kicked a rock and chose the longer path home. How could Mary make up such a story—and yet appear so sincere? *He tugged his beard.* How could I have been so wrong about her? Is she deranged, or have I been the crazy one?

LIFE HAS ITS IRONIES, AND SO DOES MATTHEW'S LIST OF WOMEN named in Jesus' genealogy. Each woman we've studied had to overcome some overwhelming handicap. Ruth came from a pagan culture with an anti-Semitic history. Tamar and Bathsheba were involved in sex scandals. Rahab was a prostitute. What could taint pure Mary's reputation? The virgin birth—the very symbol of God's special favor—brought ridicule on Mary, Joseph, and Jesus.

Satan's workers masquerade as "angels of light." They appear faultless. But God's servants are often rough around the edges. They are real, not airbrushed fakes.

Jesus' mother, Mary, is the most familiar of the women named in Jesus' genealogy. While some Catholics have adored her, many Protestants have ignored her. The Bible shows an amazing woman worthy of our respect and aware of her need for a Savior. Her name means "their rebellion." The Jews were under the tyranny of Roman occupation during her lifetime. We find many women called Mary in the New Testament. Perhaps the name was popular for Jewish girls because of their oppression.

This Mary turned that meaning upside down. Portraits and statues of the Madonna capture a vision of serenity that fits the biblical portrait very well. Far from being rebellious, Mary is a picture of perfect surrender and submission to God. We often find Mary pondering the extraordinary events surrounding Jesus' birth and life. Her contemplative nature did not translate into indecisiveness. Far from it: she was quick to surrender to God, his plan, and his warnings, even when she must have had many questions, concerns, and fears.

She remained steadfast in her faith even when God's calling meant probable public shame, possible alienation from her fiancé, and a midnight flight to a foreign country. She didn't argue like Moses, run like Jonah, or try to help God like Sarah. She surrendered, absolutely and completely, to God's personal plan for her life.

God entrusted teenaged Mary with the privilege and burden of bearing and raising his Son. Her heart will be pierced when she witnesses her blameless firstborn being mocked, shamed, and crucified. There will be no ram in the thicket to save her Son the way God spared Abraham's son. Mary's Son is the Lamb of God who takes away the sins of the world. But she will rejoice at his miraculous resurrection and witness the birth of the church.

Mary's surrender to God's plan produced serenity. Have you found that place of rest for your heart? Ask God to reveal the secret of surrender and serenity as you study Mary.

Day One
The God of the Impossible

Being a small-town, poor teenager didn't knock Mary off of God's radar. He not only knew her address, he knew her history, her heart, and her unique role in his story.

Most of us are familiar with Mary's encounter with the angel Gabriel. But imagine being Mary. How would you react if a real angel visited you? Mary claimed the great King David as an ancestor, but she wasn't even from the kingly line. What had she done to garner God's attention?

Scripture Reading...
LUKE 1:26–38

Study and Reflection

1. What impresses you about Mary's meeting with the angel and her response to his news?

2. How did Mary demonstrate her trust and surrender to God (Luke 1:38)?

3. What was Mary's part and what was God's part in fulfilling God's plan (Luke 1:34–38)?

4. What role or challenges are you facing that seem too difficult for you?

5. What difference would it make if we, like Mary, focused on the Holy Spirit's adequacy instead of our limitations when we faced challenges?

6. What does Luke 1:37 NASB, "For nothing will be impossible with God," mean for your situation?

Mysteries—Beyond Understanding

God gave Mary a humanly impossible assignment. How could she, a virgin, create a child? She couldn't. And God didn't expect her to—he was telling Mary what he would do through her.

When God calls us, he already knows how he will achieve his plan. He does not expect us to figure out the impossible. His Holy Spirit works through us, and he receives the glory. Mystery of mysteries, God uses frail human vessels to accomplish his will.

Mary didn't try to figure out how to succeed in her assignment. She knew God would accomplish his will through her. When we believe it's up to us to solve our problems, overcome an obstacle, or accomplish the impossible, we become frazzled and overwhelmed. When we trust God to accomplish his will through us, we have peace.

Do you believe God is bigger than your challenge? Knowing the God of the impossible is the first step to serenity.

I Want to Remember . . .

Write down any statements from today's lesson that will help you recall what God is teaching you. Let's encourage each other by sharing them on Twitter with the following hashtag: #LittleWomenBigGod

Today's takeaways from #LittleWomenBigGod are:

Day Two
God's Servant

"I am the Lord's servant," Mary answered. "May your word to me be fulfilled" (Luke 1:38).

The stigma of illegitimacy followed Jesus throughout his life (John 8:41). In our morally lax society, we can't fully appreciate the shame this label carried in Mary's culture. If you're familiar with books written just a century ago, you get a better idea. A compromising letter was enough to ostracize a woman from polite society, let alone an unwed pregnancy.

But Mary cared more about what God knew to be true about her than about people's gossip. Paul echoed her sentiment in Galatians 1:10, "Am I now trying to win the approval of human beings, or of God? Or am I trying to please people? If I were still trying to please people, I would not be a servant of Christ."

Mary must have had many questions: "What will Joseph think? Will I lose him? What will this do to my reputation? Will

I be shunned? Will I be stoned?" But she didn't place conditions or require assurances before accepting God's plan for her.

Mary called herself "the Lord's servant." "Servant" comes from the Greek word *doulos* and means "bondslave," or "a slave who is devoted to the interests of his master to the extent that he disregards his own interests."[1] It was a permanent relationship based on the servant's desire. "I am the Lord's servant. May it be to me as you have said."

Scripture Reading...

LUKE 1:38–56

Study and Reflection

1. If you were Mary, what questions and concerns might you have had after the angel's visit?

2. What reservations keep you from complete surrender to God's Word and will for your life?

3. How does knowing God's character calm your concerns?

4. Elizabeth's unborn child leaped for joy at the sound of Mary's voice (Luke 1:41–44). What does that tell you about the life a pregnant woman carries in her body?

5. For what does Elizabeth commend Mary (Luke 1:45)?

6. From the following, why is faith important? "And without faith it is impossible to please God, because anyone who comes to him must believe that he exists and that he rewards those who earnestly seek him" (Heb. 11:6).

7. The angel told Mary her older cousin Elizabeth was pregnant. An angel had told Zacharias, Elizabeth's husband, that their son would be the forerunner of the Messiah. Now the Holy Spirit reveals to Elizabeth that Mary is carrying the Christ. Why do you think the Lord wanted each woman to know of the other's miracle (Luke 1:17, 36, 39–45)?

8. Mary called God her Savior (Luke 1:47). Putting this with the following Scriptures, does the Bible teach that Mary was sinless? Why or why not? "As it is written: 'There is no one righteous, not even one.' . . . For all have sinned and fall short of the glory of God" (Rom. 3:10, 23).

9. From Mary's song (Luke 1:46–55), how would you describe her relationship with God and her response to being chosen for a daunting assignment?

Song of Praise

Jesus sent his disciples out in pairs. God brought Mary and Elizabeth together to share the joy and wonder of their unique miracles. This, no doubt, strengthened Mary before she had to tell Joseph she was pregnant.

God has made us to need each other. We double our joys and bolster our faith when we share our hopes, doubts, and sorrows with people who understand.

Mary's song of praise, called Mary's Magnificat, quotes the Old Testament at least fifteen times. At a young age—possibly only fifteen years old—Mary knew the Scriptures. Her spiritual foundation prepared her for God's assignment. She expressed no apprehension. We hear her joy and wonder that God would choose her for this role in his plan.

While ministering to a group of believers behind the Iron Curtain, I mentioned, through a translator, how challenging raising a perfect child must have been for Mary, an ordinary young woman. My hostess declared Mary was sinless like Jesus. While some have elevated Mary to a level of sinless perfection, Mary recognized her need for a Savior.

Mary is special not because she was given a nature better than the rest of us. She's extraordinary because in spite of her humanness she practiced unwavering faith. Mary demonstrated the poise available for us in emotionally challenging times. A servant has to please only her master. What other people think about us doesn't matter. *Lord, help us live like Mary!*

I Want to Remember . . .

Today's takeaways from #LittleWomenBigGod are:

Day Three
Misunderstood

I know God's ways are better than mine. That is, until I face roadblocks. Then I'm sure my plan is better.

Who can blame Joseph for doubting Mary's story? Mary's news that she was three months pregnant, following her abrupt visit to her cousin, would jar any man. If I'd been directing these events, I would have sent the angel to Joseph first. Why not pre-empt this tension and misunderstanding? Joseph, the designated head of their house, probably felt God should have told him first, too. Since he hadn't heard from God at this time, how could he believe Mary?

God's ways are better, but they can be confusing. God set the bar for moral standards. Why would he allow people to believe highly favored Mary was sexually immoral, when in truth she and Joseph showed great restraint? Joseph kept her a virgin until after Jesus' birth.

That must have confused Mary, too. This disgraceful repu-tation could have ruined Joseph's carpentry business, since he worked among religious Jewish patrons. Perhaps this misunder-standing gave the couple compassion for those who would not believe their story and for others misjudged by society. Because of it, we get a glowing example from Joseph of the godly way to respond to betrayal. He had a biblical right to divorce, but he chose not to shame Mary in the process.

Maybe God allowed the misunderstanding for you and me. When people believe lies about us, it hurts. What a comfort to know some of God's most highly favored saints were misunder-stood. Whatever God's reason, we know the couple themselves experienced another example of God being greater than their impossible situation. God was able to convince Joseph of Mary's faithfulness and purity.

God was building Mary and Joseph's faith for steeper chal-lenges. In the next impossible situation, they would be able to look back and remember—nothing is impossible with God. Eternity shows our heavenly Father always knows best.

Scripture Reading..

LUKE 1:38–40, 56

MATTHEW 1:18–25

Study and Reflection

1. Why do you think Mary went to stay with her cousin Elizabeth instead of running to Joseph with Gabriel's message?

2. After spending three months with Elizabeth, Mary was ready to face Joseph. Even though Mary had done nothing wrong, she had to wonder if Joseph would believe her. How did Joseph respond to Mary's news (Matt. 1:18–19)?

3. Why did Joseph decide to divorce Mary quietly instead of shaming her in front of the whole Jewish community (Matt. 1:19)?

4. God is never late, but his rescues often cut too close for comfort. How did God rescue Mary and Joseph from this terrible strain (Matt. 1:20)?

5. Mary and Joseph were separately told to name the baby Jesus, "because he will save his people from their sins" (Matt. 1:21; Luke 1:31). How could these messages, given at different times, have helped the couple?

6. Perhaps the angel reminded Joseph that God was fulfilling his word spoken through the ancient prophet in Isaiah 7:14, "Therefore the Lord himself will give you a sign: The virgin will conceive and give birth to a son, and will call him Immanuel."

   a. In Matthew 1:24–25, what does Joseph's response to the dream reveal about him?

   b. What did Joseph risk by taking Mary, who was now three months pregnant, as his wife?

7. How do the questions and disapproving attitudes of others affect your commitment to courageously walk with Jesus?

The New Testament Jewish Marriage Process

Sometimes Mary is called Joseph's wife. Other times the Scripture calls the couple engaged. Which is it?

The English word "wife" in our New Testament passages is the Greek word *gynē*. It can refer to a woman of any age—virgin, married, or widowed. The word can also mean a betrothed woman. Jesus used the same word to address Mary at the wedding in Cana (John 2:4) and from the cross (John 19:26). In the New Testament, *gynē* is translated 129 times as "woman" and 92 times as "wife."[2]

There is no contradiction when Matthew 1:24 says Joseph immediately took her as his wife, and Luke 2:5 says they were engaged when the time came to give birth. Mary was his *gynē*—virgin fiancée. The same is true for the biblical word translated "husband" in Matthew 1:19. It can mean a male, a husband, a betrothed, or future husband.[3]

In *The Indescribable Gift*, Richard Exley explains the three steps in a Jewish marriage. First there was the engagement, a contract arranged by family members. Next came the betrothal, "a public ratification of the engagement." According to Exley, "during this period the couple is considered husband and wife, though the marriage has not been consummated. The only way a betrothal could be terminated was by death or divorce. A young woman whose fiancé dies during this period is called 'a virgin who is a widow.'

"The last stage is the marriage proper, when the groom takes his bride into the bridal chamber and consummates the marriage. This is followed by a wedding party."[4]

Since Joseph did not have sexual relations with Mary until after Jesus' birth, there would have been no marriage proper and wedding party for Mary and Joseph. Tongues wagged when Joseph took Mary to live with him after she was at least three months pregnant. Rumors of illegitimacy dogged Jesus even as an adult (John 8:41). Joseph needed a visit from an angel to convince him of Mary's innocence. How could they expect their parents and community to understand?

The couple that exercised extraordinary self-control—no sex while living together for six months—was branded as not being able to control themselves. Did Joseph's business suffer because of this misunderstanding?

So few understood that God was fulfilling what he had foretold hundreds of years earlier (Matt. 1:23, quoting Isa. 7:14). Throughout Jesus' ministry, his worst critics were the religious leaders, the ones we would hope would understand. Sometimes walking with God is lonely. His call may be clear to us, but others who have not heard the call don't understand.

How Do I Handle Betrayal?

Remember how Judah responded when he heard Tamar was pregnant? He demanded she be dragged out and burned. Judah was quick to punish and publicly shame Tamar even though he shared her guilt.

How different Joseph's response was. Mary had unexpectedly left town for three months. When she returned with the news, "I am pregnant, but it is not what you think. I am carrying the Messiah," Joseph was devastated. Perhaps he wondered how she could concoct such a lie to cover her unfaithfulness. But even in the midst of his churning emotions, his righteous character guided him to sever the relationship in a gracious and private manner. While he considered this, the angel showed up and stopped him.

I've noticed those who are quick to expose and shame others (like Judah) often harbor their own dirty secrets. It's as if they believe a public display of indignation will absolve them of their own guilt. Showing others they know right from wrong does not make them right before God. In fact, they condemn themselves. They show they did the very wrong they now condemn in others.

Joseph models a Christlike response to betrayal. Kindness and grace leave the door open for the wrongdoer to repent and be restored to God and his people. In Joseph's case, when Mary's reputation was cleared, he had to deal only with having doubted her story. He had no regrets about how he had handled the matter.

I Want to Remember . . .

Today's takeaways from #LittleWomenBigGod are:

Unmet Expectations

Caesar Augustus demanded taxes. He didn't care if collecting them inconvenienced old men or pregnant women. For an official census, thousands of families had to travel for days or longer to their native cities. These difficult trips were not only made at personal expense, they meant days without income. Was God surprised? No. He had written the story and now directed the cast. He had chosen the small town Bethlehem for his Son's birth (Micah 5:2). So he channeled his plans through this monarch to make sure Mary was there to deliver Jesus (Prov. 21:1). This fulfilled one of over three hundred prophecies that were realized by Jesus' first coming.

Scripture Reading...

MICAH 5:2
But you, Bethlehem Ephrathah, though you are small among the clans of Judah, out of you will come for me one who will be ruler over Israel, whose origins are from of old, from ancient times.

PROVERBS 21:1 NLT
The king's heart is like a stream of water directed by the LORD; he guides it wherever he pleases.

LUKE 2:1–20

Study and Reflection

1. What situation has recently caused you aggravation and seemingly meaningless bother and expense?

2. How does God's sovereignty in this expensive inconvenience for Mary and Joseph help you look at your difficulties?

3. If you were carrying a king's child, what provisions might you expect the king to provide for his only son's birth?

4. How did God provide (Luke 2:1–20)?

5. Isaiah 55:8–9 says, "For my thoughts are not your thoughts, neither are your ways my ways," declares the LORD. "As the heavens are higher than the earth, so are my ways higher than your ways and my thoughts than your thoughts."

   a. What does this tell you about God's ways in contrast to our human ways?

   b. How does this verse convey whose ways are better?

6. Think of an area where God has not provided in the way you had hoped. Knowing that God has your best in mind, how do you deal with unmet expectations?

7. The day each of our two children was born, I phoned family members across the continent. "Our baby has arrived!" Parents often send out birth announcements. Who sent out Jesus' birth announcement and how (Luke 2:8–14)?

8. Consider to whom a great king and head of the faith might send a birth announcement.

    a. Who did God tell about Christ's birth?

    b. Who did he leave out?

Unrealistic Expectations

If you were pregnant with the king's child, wouldn't you anticipate some special treatment? If an angel said you were highly favored of God, wouldn't you expect a few easy breaks?

When Larry and I began our family, we were living in Orange County, California, the most expensive housing market in the United States at the time. This was during the years of sky-high inflation. We were paying 18 percent interest on our home mortgage. In other words, we were house-poor. Our sixty-year-old, eight-hundred-square-foot house was anything but luxurious, but our monthly mortgage payments drained us dry. I admit I sometimes felt sorry for myself because I couldn't afford to buy my new baby the cute things I admired.

Mary's story jarred me from my self-pity. She didn't even have a clean room in which to deliver her infant. She wrapped her baby in strips of cloth. Herod the king wanted to kill her Son. Suddenly my situation didn't look so bad. I covered secondhand bumper pads with fresh yellow gingham and painted a used crib. Friends brought by used plantation shutters that fit the windows as if they were custom-made for them. The nursery sparkled.

I had to climb one flight of steps while in labor, but Mary had to walk or, at best, ride a donkey for miles. If such conditions were adequate for the Son of the Most High, who was I to complain? Mary's story challenged my attitude and rescued me from unrealistic expectations.

Great Expectations

If I'd been Mary, I would have expected a bit of pampering—at least a private room, a bed with clean linens, and a midwife. Mary could have focused on her hardships. Who gave birth in an animal stable without any family to comfort or celebrate with her? Like Prissy in *Gone with the Wind*, Joseph probably didn't know nothin' 'bout birthing babies.

Isaiah 55:9 says God's ways are higher than our ways. We know that higher is better. Think higher grades, higher quality, or higher value. God's ways aren't just a little better; they are immeasurably better as the heavens are higher than the earth.

How could "no room for them in the inn" be better (Luke 2:7)? The inn may have been a guest room in someone's home or a walled-in area around a well without the private suites we'd expect. I picture a hurricane shelter filled with cots and bedrolls. People would mill around and surely gawk at a woman giving birth.

The manger became the sign that identified Jesus to the shepherds. He was the only baby that night in a manger. The stable or cave that held the manger provided Mary and Joseph privacy the packed inn would have lacked. It also offered a quiet place for the shepherds to visit and worship the infant Christ.

If Joseph and Mary's families had believed their story, Mary might have stayed behind. Their lack of support made sure she was in Bethlehem. Their doubts, if they had been with her, would have been a distraction, not a comfort. God chose shepherds to share their wonder and angels to celebrate with the couple. God didn't meet my expectations of how to care for the mother of his Son. He did exceedingly better.

Sometimes we fail to appreciate God's perfect provisions for our lives because we're looking for something different. Birthdays, anniversaries, Mother's Day, and Valentine's Day all arrive with ideas of how *we* should be treated. Expectations inflict unnecessary pain and affect our relationships.

What assumptions are you putting on yourself and others? How would surrendering those expectations relieve your disappointment? How would believing that God wants the very best for you and is sovereignly ruling over all the circumstances of your life affect your attitude and gratitude?

I Want to Remember . . .

Today's takeaways from #LittleWomenBigGod are:

Day Five
Provision

One of my favorite quotes from Amy Carmichael's book *If* is: "If the praise of others elates me and their blame depresses me; if I cannot rest under misunderstanding without defending myself; if I love to be loved more than to love, to be served more than to serve, then I know nothing of Calvary love." Mary showed the humility that comes from knowing God's love.

Mary was honored by her role, despite the obstacles. She didn't doubt God's love for her or his Son when she couldn't afford to offer a lamb for him. Knowing God's love helps us value whatever part we play in his story. We trust that his provision is eternally better for our story than the best the world can offer.

Scripture Reading...

Luke 2:21–40

LEVITICUS 12:8
If she cannot afford a lamb, she is to bring two doves or two young pigeons, one for a burnt offering and the other for a sin offering. In this way the priest will make atonement for her, and she will be clean.

Study and Reflection

1. What does Mary and Joseph's offering tell you about their financial status?

2. How can Mary and Joseph's simple offering at Jesus' "baby dedication" help couples when they can't afford to give their children the world's best?

3. What do Simeon's Spirit-empowered words reveal about Jesus' role for both Jews and Gentiles (Luke 2:25–32)?

4. What does Simeon tell Mary will happen to her (Luke 2:34–35)?

5. No mention is made of either Mary or Joseph's parents. John 19:25 lets us know Mary had a sister, but her sister is not mentioned as being present during this momentous period. How

could Simeon and Anna's words have been a blessing to Mary throughout her life (Luke 2:29–38)?

6. When have you experienced the body of Christ being a family to you?

When You Face the Impossible . . . Lessons from Mary

One morning after a series of unpleasant twists in my life, I discovered that one of my favorite French chairs was coming apart. At the sight, I came unglued. But this event had a positive result. Like lancing an infected boil, all my fears and confusion spewed out. I was able to get down to business with the Lord. He cleaned out my infection and exposed some idols that had crept into my heart. This reminded me that brokenness and surrender are the only avenues to real peace.

God granted me the grace to say, "It all belongs to you. I don't understand why you're allowing these things in our lives, but I surrender all to you." A simple but powerful prayer.

By nature, I am a fighter and fixer of what I care about. If something is wrong, I want to make it right. In some circumstances that may be good, but sometimes the need to act can turn into a power struggle with God. Sometimes God allows things I cannot mend to invade my world so I'll remember I don't know best. I'm not in control. Pull out the white flag; *Lord, you are my captain. I surrender to your good, acceptable, and perfect will* (Rom. 8:28).

Cognitively, I believe God is in charge and his will is perfect, but I don't always feel it. I know when I get to heaven I'll be amazed at his wisdom. When I finally *see* things from his perspective, I will worship, not complain. But now I must draw on my faith to remember these truths.

Surrender Brings Serenity

The best part of surrendering is that after you've surrendered everything, there is nothing left to worry about. I believe this was the secret of Mary's serenity. Remember her words, "I am the Lord's servant. May it be to me as you have said" (Luke 1:38).

Because she was totally surrendered, she could gracefully walk through the story God had for her.

- Mary surrendered her body and her reputation, even though doing so brought misunderstanding and slander.
- Mary surrendered her relationship with Joseph, even though surrendering could have meant divorce and single parenthood.
- Mary surrendered her right to a proper wedding and marriage celebration, even though she'd probably looked forward to one, and without one she could be shunned.
- Mary surrendered her expectations and safety, even though it meant inconvenience and heartache.

The irony of humility and surrender is after we surrender, we become channels of his love. Mary received the honor of being the mother of God's Son, and in so doing she blessed the entire human race. She is still honored throughout the whole world.

Serenity is the fruit of surrender, but surrender must be renewed continually. New challenges expose substitutes for God in our lives. Each renewal brings satisfying peace that is better than all the comforts and treasures of the world.

What gets in the way of your surrender to God? Do you question his love for you? What unreliable sources have you looked to for peace? It is easy to believe that if I only had financial security, were more efficient, had a fulfilling career, wore a smaller size, or had a different mate, new friend, or better health—then I would be happy and at peace. Why not offer your false gods back to God and watch him work?

Mary was a person with genuine needs and emotions. Despite her youthfulness, she had the character and depth of a seasoned saint. Grounded in Scripture and buoyed by her faith, Mary accepted the life given to her. Like Prince Caspian in the Chronicles of Narnia series, if this were the adventure God had for her, then she would see it through. As she embraced God's plan—including the unfathomable—she experienced the impossible. With God, nothing is impossible.

I Want to Remember . . .

Today's takeaways from #LittleWomenBigGod are:

Prayer Requests

Record your small group's prayer requests here.

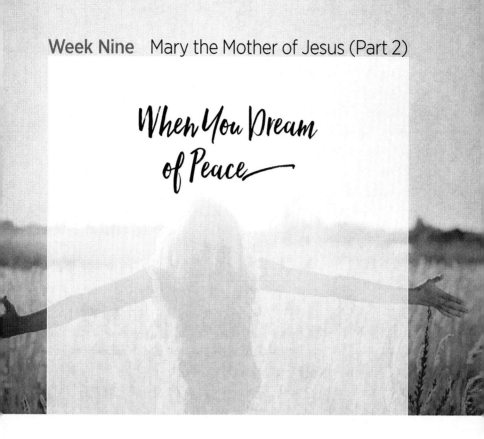

When You Dream of Peace

I REMEMBER DADDY MARCHING DOWN THE CHURCH AISLE AT Christmas, singing, "We three kings of Orient are . . ." My childhood view of Christmas was colorful, clean, and pleasant. I had a sanitized view of camels, too—until I visited one at Mount Vernon. Their resident camel was filthy, by his own choice. He sometimes projected his bodily excretions in the direction of onlookers. My romantic view of a stable and the three wise men's journey vanished.

Gone also is the childhood notion that the first Christmas was all joy and peace for the main characters. Mary and Joseph experienced a bevy of emotions and challenges that included betrayal, fear, and loneliness. But there was peace and joy, too. Mary continues to amaze me with her peacefulness in the midst of upheaval.

Today's lesson begins with a visit from the magi. Traveling at a camel's pace, the journey from the East to Bethlehem took a long time, perhaps over a year. They come to worship the King of the Jews, but their visit will also stir up trouble for Mary and her little family.

Day One
Resilience

Talk about miserable—imagine being eight to nine months pregnant and traveling over rough roads on the swaying back of a donkey or by foot. But Mary chose the inconvenience of traveling with Joseph over staying in Nazareth.

After Jesus' birth, the couple appears to have settled in Bethlehem. Mary's out-of-wedlock pregnancy had kept Nazareth's gossipers busy. Now something worse than raised eyebrows and cold shoulders will force another move.

Herod was a tyrant. During his reign, he had a wife and three sons killed. But because he was a Jew, he wouldn't eat a pig. Caesar Augustus reportedly quipped, "It is better to be Herod's pig than son."[1] King Herod was no ordinary madman. This paranoid ruler marshaled the equivalent of the police, National Guard, and military. The terrifying events in today's Scripture reading most likely took place after Jesus' first birthday.

When the magi came looking for the newborn "King of the Jews," Herod feigned devotion. He questioned the magi to discover when the star signifying the Messiah's birth had appeared.

He then had all the boys in Bethlehem age two and under slaughtered.

Scripture Reading..

MATTHEW 2:1–23

Study and Reflection

1. While Herod would not be inconvenienced to travel the short distance between Jerusalem and Bethlehem to see the newborn king, the magi traveled some four hundred miles by camel to see Jesus.

    a. Considering the motivation for their journey, what do these wise men teach us (Matt. 2:2)?

    b. Half the joy of a wonderful experience is being able to share it with those who celebrate with you. But who could believe and share Mary and Joseph's joy? How sweet that God continues to bring strangers to celebrate with them. How could the magi's visit have encouraged Mary and Joseph?

    c. What gifts did they present?

2. According to Matthew 2:13,16–18, what plans did Herod have for Mary's son?

3. Mary and Joseph must have been on a high after the visit of the magi. Jesus' Father had not only proclaimed his Son's coming by angels, he'd written it in the stars! But this high was soon followed by a deep low. List the messages God gave Joseph and how he responded to each warning (Matt. 2:13–15, 19–23).

4. What do Joseph's actions reveal about his relationship with God?

5. How important was it for Joseph to obey immediately? What if he had delayed until he had finished his night's sleep or taken a day to wrap up a carpentry project for a customer? What if Mary had insisted on hearing from the angel, too?

6. How do you apply his example to your life?

7. An angel warned Joseph. Today God's messages may come as quiet promptings or urgent jabs. We know God will never lead us to do anything that violates his character and his Word. How do you identify whether or not your impulses are from God?

8. Simeon had told Mary, "A sword will pierce your own soul too" (Luke 2:35). This prophecy must have haunted and perplexed her. Ultimately those words pointed to the cross. But this event pierced her even though Jesus would be spared.

Since Mary and Joseph were living in Bethlehem for a while, they must have known some of the parents who lost sons Jesus' age.

Consider Mary's emotionally charged circumstances:

- Hunted by the king's army
- Learning her son's pursuers had murdered her friends' babies

a. From what we've observed in Mary, where do you think she found the strength to endure this terrible ordeal?

b. What situations cause you stress?

c. Writing out my cares and giving them one by one to the Lord helps me when I'm stressed. What helps you handle your anxiety?

9. Being on the run put Mary and Joseph under emotional, physical, and financial stress. There was no SUV into which to toss their meager belongings. They had to carry their toddler and their belongings on foot or with the help of a donkey. There were no fast-food restaurants. Imagine the difficulty of establishing a carpentry business if you were constantly moving. From what unexpected source had God provided for this time (Matt. 2:11)?

Recognizing God's Voice

A woman came to see me who was married to an unbelieving alcoholic. He knew one verse from Scripture and used it regularly to club her into submission.

"Why are you letting an unbeliever interpret Scripture for you?" I asked.

Psalm 119:160 (NASB) says, "The sum of Your word is truth." I've seen people take one verse out of context and use it to support unbiblical actions. God's will agrees with the whole counsel of Scripture and with his heart. Beware of heeding every prompting that carries a verse. Even the devil twisted Scripture to tempt Jesus. We must test the spirit behind the promptings we receive (1 John 4:1).

Trusting God with Untimely Death

God sent an angel to warn Mary and Joseph about Herod's deadly campaign to kill Jesus. Yet while Jesus was spared, many parents lost their sons. Later, God would allow Jesus to suffer a more agonizing death on the cross.

On this side of heaven, we can't understand God's ways. We have to trust his character. Jeremiah had predicted the death of the other infants hundreds of years earlier (Matt. 2:17–18). Remembering God knew this would happen must have comforted Mary in her grief and confusion.

Mama died when I was a teenager. Knowing our time is in God's hands helps me better handle the bitter sting of death. No one could touch Jesus before his time. Neither can anyone touch any child of God without his permission. When he gives permission, it is for our eternal good and for his glory. Our story is a small part of his story, a greater story more wonderful than we can imagine.

When looking at a life that seems to have been cut short, it helps me to look at years as dollars. If you only have eighty dollars to your name and you lose fifty of them, you have suffered a tremendous loss. But if you are a billionaire and lose fifty dollars, you haven't lost much.

We were made for eternity. We are more than billionaires! Years lost here are spent in heaven. For those loved ones left here on earth, death is bitter. But knowing God never makes a mistake, that we will be united for eternity, and that he uses even evil people's actions for our good (Gen. 50:20) comforts me in confusing times.

In what confusing loss or situation do you need God's perspective and comfort? Ask him to comfort you today.

I Want to Remember . . .

Write down any statements from today's lesson that will help you recall what God is teaching you. Let's encourage each other by sharing them on Twitter with the following hashtag: #LittleWomenBigGod

Today's takeaways from #LittleWomenBigGod are:

Day Two
Reflective

Most teenage boys think they know more than their mothers do. Mary's son actually did. Her firstborn was her Creator. Jesus had shaped the planets and hung the stars (Heb. 1:2). He'd painted Mary's eyes and fashioned her frame while she was in his grandmother's womb.

Jesus increased in wisdom as he grew. This means he temporarily set aside the knowledge of his prebirth history. To have the full human experience, Jesus learned like other children. As Jesus entered his teens, even in a humbled human state, he knew more than Mary and Joseph in some areas. Scripture gives us only a brief peek into this aspect of Mary's relationship with Jesus.

The process of letting go of our children begins early. The toddler squirms in our arms from a natural drive for independence. Mary's relationship with Jesus had to change in a way all parents experience with their children, only magnified. The One she carried, birthed, and raised must now take on the mission for which he had come. He would be the Savior of the world, her Lord and God.

Scripture Reading..

LUKE 2:39–52

Study and Reflection

1. What unique challenges do you think Mary faced parenting God's Son?

2. How did Mary respond to this new phase in Jesus' development (Luke 2:51)?

3. Mary treasured the details surrounding Jesus in her heart. What helps you secure the treasures of your life?

4. Remember a time when you had to lead or teach someone better informed than you.

a. What kind of leader or teacher would see that as an asset, and who would be threatened by it?

b. What does this tell you about Mary?

5. Do you think the Scripture teaches that Mary remained a virgin her whole life? Why or why not?

a. Isn't this the carpenter's son? Isn't his mother's name Mary, and aren't his brothers James, Joseph, Simon and Judas? Aren't all his sisters with us? Where then did this man get all these things? (Matt. 13:55–56)

b. Then Joseph woke up. He did exactly what God's angel commanded in the dream: He married Mary. But he did not consummate the marriage until she had the baby. (Matt. 1:24–25 *The Message*)

6. What insight into the family dynamics (after Jesus is grown) do you gain from the following verses? "Jesus' brothers said to him, 'Leave Galilee and go to Judea, so that your disciples there may see the works you do. No one who wants to become a public figure acts in secret. Since you are doing these things, show yourself to the world.' For even his own brothers did not believe in him" (John 7:3–5).

7. Mary was not sequestered in some ivory tower away from the pressures we experience. Her younger sons ridiculed Jesus.

Perhaps Jesus' brothers resented being disciplined and corrected while their older brother literally could do no wrong. How does knowing that Mary's family was not always peaceful help you in facing the tensions in your life?

Securing Our Treasures

Far from being threatened by her Son's wisdom and growing independence, Mary treasured this new phase of growth in his life. This isn't the first time Mary has treasured and pondered things in her heart (Luke 2:19). "Treasured" comes from the Greek work *syntēreō*, which means (1) to preserve (a thing from perishing or being lost), and (2) to keep within one's self, keep in mind (a thing, lest it be forgotten).[2]

Like Mary, we need to reflect on our experiences. My sister and I call this "head time." Reflection allows us to capture the feelings, memories, and lessons of life. Without quiet times of thought, we become stretched thin and overlook life's gifts. We overreact to the normal stresses of life. Pondering preserves the experiences of our lives so we can invest them in the future. These times of quiet anchor our souls in God. They enrich us with wisdom, gratitude, and insight for life.

Quiet enriches our senses. Journaling connects me with God and my thoughts. Peaceful bicycle rides and regular times of personal meditation meet this need for my husband. Experiment to find what helps you stay grounded when your world trembles.

I Want to Remember . . .

Today's takeaways from #LittleWomenBigGod are:

Yielding

Scripture is silent about Joseph's death. Because he's not mentioned after Jesus is twelve, many suppose Mary was widowed at a young age. Jesus, the eldest son, would have taken over as family provider. Joseph had shared the knowledge of Jesus' immaculate (free from original sin) conception. He had weathered the ridicule and strains surrounding Jesus' birth with Mary. Now he was gone.

Mary's other sons didn't believe Jesus was God's son. Mary learned to look to Jesus to solve the problems Joseph had shouldered earlier.

Jesus began his public ministry when he was thirty years old. At the beginning of his ministry, he attended the wedding at Cana. Mary must have been helping at the wedding. She was aware of the panic when the wine ran out.

At this wedding and at the cross (John 19:26–27), Jesus called Mary "woman," which sounds curt to us. But the tenderness of the moment of his crucifixion shows this was a respectful address. It was like saying "ma'am" or "madam."

Scripture Reading...

JOHN 2:1–11

Study and Reflection

1. What happened at the wedding in Cana, and what did Mary instinctively do (John 2:1–11)?

2. What do you learn about Mary's relationship with Jesus from this event?

3. Why do you think Mary told Jesus the wine had run out?

4. What did Mary tell the servants to do (John 2:5)?

5. How can you apply Mary's words to your life and relationship with Jesus?

6. Running out of wine was embarrassing but not a necessity for life. What does Jesus' miracle show you about his heart?

Gentle Trust

Mary's abiding trust was demonstrated again at the wedding when the wine ran out. She knew Jesus' compassion. She trusted his wisdom and ability. Perhaps Jesus had miraculously multiplied food for his family in the meager years after Joseph died. Satan certainly knew he could turn a stone into bread (Matt. 4:3).

Did you notice that she didn't tell Jesus what to do? She just told him the problem. If Mary didn't feel a need to tell her son how to solve the problem, I wonder why I think I need to come up with the solution for Jesus to execute.

Mary wasn't playing the "I'm your mother, and you need to do this for me" card. She simply trusted Jesus as she had trusted his Father when the angel told her she would bear God's child.

I Want to Remember . . .

Today's takeaways from #LittleWomenBigGod are:

Tough and Tender

My friend received one of those calls you pray you'll never get. She learned her grandson had been in a terrible car accident and rushed to the hospital. He wasn't expected to pull through. While his blood dripped on her shoes, she lovingly caressed his hand and told him how much she loved him. She refused to leave his side for even a moment while he still had breath.

Unfortunately, his parents weren't that strong. They huddled in the waiting room and occasionally darted in and out of his room. They were unable to stand by their son while his life ebbed away.

In times of intense pain, some sufferers are left alone. Their friends and family withdraw to protect themselves from the discomfort of not knowing what to say or do. They can't fix the problem, and they can't handle the pain. But that was not Mary. She was as tough as she was tender. She tenaciously stayed by Jesus until the end, even when his burly disciples fled. But prior to the cross, Mary learned to adjust to Jesus' mission. Today, we'll look at her transition and her strength at the cross.

Scripture Reading

MATTHEW 12:46–50
While Jesus was still talking to the crowd, his mother and brothers stood outside, wanting to speak to him. Someone told him, "Your mother and brothers are standing outside, wanting to speak

to you." He replied to him, "Who is my mother, and who are my brothers?" Pointing to his disciples, he said, "Here are my mother and my brothers. For whoever does the will of my Father in heaven is my brother and sister and mother." (Luke 8:19–21 is a parallel passage.)

Study and Reflection

1. At a point in his ministry, Jesus was too busy to eat. Mary's other sons didn't believe in Jesus (John 7:5). How has Mary's relationship with Jesus changed?

2. My mother-in-law once said, "You never stop being a mother—no matter how old your child is." Mary had, no doubt, looked to Jesus after Joseph died. She may have been torn between wanting to take care of Jesus and missing time with him. What can you learn from Jesus' response that could help you in your relationships with your parents or with your adult children?

3. How can you apply Jesus' example when important relation-ships threaten to hinder you from God's calling?[3]

4. Who is trying to interfere with your following God's unique path for your life?

5. Now we turn to the cross. From the following verses, where was Mary at Jesus' crucifixion? What does that tell you about her? "Near the cross of Jesus stood his mother, his mother's sister, Mary the wife of Clopas, and Mary Magdalene. When Jesus saw his mother there, and the disciple whom he loved standing nearby, he said to his mother, 'Dear woman, here is your son,' and to the disciple, 'Here is your mother.' From that time on, this disciple took her into his home" (John 19:25–27 NIV 1984).

6. What did Jesus do when he saw his mother?

7. Our final view of Mary follows Jesus' ascension into heaven. "When they arrived, they went upstairs to the room where they were staying. Those present were Peter, John, James and Andrew; Philip and Thomas, Bartholomew and Matthew; James son of Alphaeus and Simon the Zealot, and Judas son of James. They all joined together constantly in prayer, along with the women and Mary the mother of Jesus, and with his brothers" (Acts 1:13–14).

   a. What seems to be Mary's new role?

   b. Who else in Mary's family was present?

Resilience

Jesus' calling from his Father took precedence over his human family's desires. His laser focus on his mission meant Mary no longer had immediate access to him. This was another adjustment for Mary.

Many adults struggle with how to honor their father and mother and take care of their own spouse and children. Does honoring mean obeying their wishes or being available to their every need?

Jesus was single, yet he modeled a respectful separation. He did not dishonor his mother when he was unavailable to her. His Father was his Lord. At the cross, Jesus made sure his mother would be taken care of on earth. He knew the difference between Mary's legitimate needs and desires that would sidetrack him from his mission.

Mary adapted. She remembered his words to her when he was only twelve, "Why were you looking for me? Didn't you know that I had to be here, dealing with the things of my Father?" (Luke 2:49 *The Message*)

Unfading Beauty

Mary showed the unfading beauty of a quiet and gentle spirit that is precious to God (1 Pet. 3:3–4). God knew when he sent Gabriel to Mary what kind of girl he'd find. He knew Mary would trust him—all the way to the cross. Because Mary knew God and cherished his Word in her heart, her faith did not die when a sword pierced her own heart.

Jesus said, "My sheep listen to my voice; I know them, and they follow me" (John 10:27). God knew Mary would follow him through the challenges required to be the mother of his Son. She did. May the same be true of us.

I Want to Remember . . .

Today's takeaways from #LittleWomenBigGod are:

Day Five
Ageless

We've walked with Mary through her encounter with the angel, Joseph's unbelief, her giving birth in an animal stable, being hunted down by an army, being widowed, releasing Jesus to fulfill his mission, watching Jesus' crucifixion, and praying for the birth of the church. Reflect back on her life and how God showed himself strong on her behalf.

Application and Reflection

1. What impressed you the most in how Mary faced her challenges and lived her life?

2. Mary experienced challenges similar to the ones we face. She was misunderstood; falsely accused; had to trust her husband's leading; felt she knew what was best for her grown son; and dealt with sibling rivalry among her children. What helped you identify with Mary and see her as a real person?

3. What do you learn about God from Mary's story?

4. How has Mary challenged your thinking?

5. What changes are you prompted to make in your life?

When You Dream of Peace . . . More Lessons from Mary

"And a sword will pierce your own soul too." Not the kind of words you expect to receive at your baby's dedication. The words sent cold chills down Mary's spine. *Too! What did Simeon mean?*

Over her life, Simeon's words haunted her. Times such as when Joseph woke her in the dead of night, "Mary! Mary, get up! We must leave at once." Or when news reached her ears of the baby boys Herod's swords had pierced—children killed by the ones seeking her son. But Simeon's words were never more relevant than when she watched Jesus being mocked, scourged, and crucified.

Mary knew Jesus in ways no other human could. She'd witnessed his blameless character since his birth. She knew his devotion to his Father. She could endure *her* character being wrongly judged, but to watch her beloved son suffer on the cross as a common criminal pierced clear through her soul.

Yet through every trial, Mary displayed the unfading beauty of a gentle and quiet spirit. Let's look at the beautiful qualities that allowed Mary to experience peace in the midst of pain and confusion.

Resilience

Mary was resilient. She endured personal scorn, threats, poverty, and her son's crucifixion with remarkable poise and dignity. Her experiences honed her character to rely on God's grace. Each impossible situation only proved again—nothing is too big for God.

Tenacity

When her government and religious leaders sentenced her blameless son to a criminal's death, most of Jesus' disciples fled. But Mary planted herself at his feet. She stuck with Jesus from his first breath to his final gasp.

Adaptability

Mary was the only mother to experience raising a perfect child. When other mothers complained of the "terrible twos" or challenging teen years, Mary could only savor the wonder of living with a sinless human. Even after Jesus' understanding surpassed hers and Joseph's, Mary saw Jesus humbly submit to their lead until the time came for him to take on the mission for which he'd come.

When Jesus began his ministry, Mary had to adjust to a new relationship with her son. She had lived with the Prince of Peace under her roof. The living Word was there to answer her questions concerning the Scriptures and life. What an emptiness his departure must have left.

To switch roles from protecting an offspring to releasing him or her can be tricky. Jesus must have lived with Mary until he began his public ministry. Mary's transition was significantly more complicated than releasing an adult son; she had to switch from calling him "Son" to calling him "Savior and God."

Mary successfully adapted to her new role in her relationship with Christ. She gathered with Jesus' disciples and prayed to her Son and her God. Mary, no doubt, supplied Luke with the personal details of Jesus' birth (Luke 1:2-3).

Unwavering Trust

I believe God welcomes our questions. But Mary astonishes me by only asking how instead of why. She never questioned God in all her hardships. As God's bondservant, she trusted him with whatever he allowed.

Mary made regular deposits into her faith. We don't expect money to be in a bank account when we need it if we've never deposited funds. Likewise, we can't expect faith and character to be available when trials come if we haven't made regular deposits. How many times do we see Mary "pondering" in her heart? Mary made a conscious effort to hold on to God's truths and the lessons she was learning. Knowing God's character provided peace when life didn't make sense.

True Peace

Mary didn't know an angel would appear one day with an impossible assignment. Yet when he did, she never questioned *if* God could impregnate a virgin. She didn't fret over the possible challenges. She worshipped God and marveled at his grace. She didn't know her king would try to murder her baby. Her deposits of faith had shaped a character able to bear up under each unexpected trial with poise and grace.

That kind of inner beauty is cultivated one day at a time, one decision at a time, and one discipline after another. "Arrow prayers," the quick "Lord, help me" prayers, are handy in a crisis. But the clear eye, strong arms, and steady faith needed to carry us through real trials are honed through intentional connections with God.

What are you doing to cultivate your relationship with God? Every decision we make is woven into the fabric of our character. Inner peace begins with a personal relationship with God through his Son, Jesus, and grows as we nurture our relationship with him.

Do you know that nothing is impossible with Jesus? If not, you won't be able to have Mary's serene spirit when trials come.

Have you chosen to be his bondservant? If so, then you can give up solving overwhelming problems. You only need to follow his lead.

What small, daily habits could you add to your routine to cultivate the peace you found in Mary? Are you becoming a woman whom God could trust with a special assignment for his kingdom?

During the last two weeks, you have learned more about the mother of Jesus. Make it your life's aim to truly know and walk with her Son, and you too will enjoy the inner serenity Mary knew.

I Want to Remember . . .

Today's takeaways from #LittleWomenBigGod are:

Prayer Requests

Record your small group's prayer requests here.

When You Gotta Tell Somebody

"How beautiful are the feet that bring good news."

DID YOU ENJOY LEARNING ABOUT THE WOMEN FROM JESUS' genealogy? Most of us are intrigued with our family trees. It's interesting when we get insights into our family line. The women we studied are not only a part of Jesus' history but also are our ancestors in the faith.

God uses the stories of ordinary people to impact others in a big way. Did you realize that your story could draw someone closer to Christ? When you draw your final breath, I'm sure you'll want to leave with the assurance that you'll be reunited with your loved ones in heaven. Your story of faith is one of your best tools to point them to Christ.

This week's lesson will prepare you to share the hope you have in Christ (1 Pet. 3:15). If you are doing this study in a group, I know you'll enjoy hearing how God has worked in each other's lives. At the end of this lesson, I share my story.

Use the questions on the following pages to organize your history of faith into a story you can share with others as Rahab did with her family. I think you will be encouraged as you recall how God has worked in your life.

If the following questions cause you to question whether you've ever joined God's family, let this be your invitation to faith.

Invitations require a response. A friend's child struggled with decisions when she was young. That tendency denied her some wonderful opportunities. Desirable elective classes at school would fill up while she deliberated. Invariably she would have to settle for what was left. Indecision made her decision and closed the door to what she wanted. Don't let that be you. Accept Christ's invitation to eternal life.

Others may know they're in the family but don't recall the specific time they were "born again" (John 3:3). Ask the Holy Spirit to help you remember your spiritual history. Drawing out a timeline and noting your spiritual landmarks may help. The first time I did this exercise, I had a hard time pinning down the time of my rebirth. I remembered a few aha moments. But as I worked on it, the time of my spiritual birth became clearer. Don't get hung up if you don't recall the details.

This is your personal journey; it won't look like someone else's. I have two times of significant transition in my spiritual journey. When I am talking with someone, I highlight the parts that relate to my listener.

The questions that follow are to help you think through and arrange your experiences into a story you can share. You are more likely to use a concise version than a long one. Three minutes is enough to whet someone's appetite. After you answer the questions, write your story out in a continuous flow. You may want to think of an attention-grabbing question, quote, or statement to begin your story. Consider ending with a Scripture that sums up your spiritual history or continues to influence your life.

Here is a suggested prayer to help you begin.

Dear Father,
Thank you for revealing yourself to me. How amazing to receive a new identity and a holy calling to represent you in the world. Thank you for Jesus and the price he paid to save me from the emptiness and mistakes of my past, from condemnation in this life and the next, and for his daily power to save me from temptations. Please remind me of how you have worked in my life. Guide me as I organize my thoughts. Grant me the grace and courage to share the wonderful story of your amazing grace in my life with those you bring across my path. In Jesus' name. Amen.

Day One
My Life Before Christ

The apostle Paul shared his testimony before kings. When you read it today, notice how he begins by describing his life before he came to faith in Christ. He then tells of his conversion experience and transformation.

Scripture Reading...

1 PETER 2:9–10
But you are a chosen people, a royal priesthood, a holy nation, God's special possession, that you may declare the praises of him

who called you out of darkness into his wonderful light. Once you were not a people, but now you are the people of God; once you had not received mercy, but now you have received mercy.

ACTS 26:1–29

Reflection and Application

What were you like before God brought you into his light? Describe your life or mind-set before you met Christ. Were you afraid of dying or of the future? Were you self-assured or insecure? Were you driven or aimless?

Rahab was a harlot, but we aren't given the details of her sinful past. Paul was a persecutor of the church. The detail he shares highlights his transformation and God's grace. You're setting the background to spotlight Christ and show the difference he has made in your attitudes, thinking, and behavior.

I Want to Remember . . .

Write down any statements from today's lesson that will help you recall what God is teaching you. Let's encourage each other by sharing them on Twitter with the following hashtag: #LittleWomenBigGod

Today's takeaways from #LittleWomenBigGod are:

Day Two
My Turning Point

Rahab heard the stories about the God of Israel. She was curious and invited the spies in when they appeared at her door. When she was faced with turning them over to the authorities, she boldly decided to unite with them. Recall the events that led up to your salvation and spurred you to follow Christ.

Scripture Reading..

JOHN 1:12
Yet to all who did receive him, to those who believed in his name, he gave the right to become children of God.

REVELATION 3:20
Here I am! I stand at the door and knock. If anyone hears my voice and opens the door, I will come in and eat with that person, and they with me.

Reflection

Describe your turning point. What happened to create a thirst for God? When and how did you hear him knocking at your heart's door? What situations precipitated the light coming on for you and your welcoming him into your life?

Perhaps your coming to personal faith was not as dramatic as Rahab's. If your history is more like Mary's, where you grew up among followers of Christ, when did your faith become personal? When did it move from your head to your heart?

I Want to Remember . . .

Today's takeaways from #LittleWomenBigGod are:

Day Three
My New Life

Some of us experienced dramatic changes that were obvious to all around us. For others, the changes were gradual and subtle. But there were changes.

Maybe you gained joy and peace or a new sense of purpose. You may have shed your self-consciousness or former passions. Perhaps you were no longer afraid of dying, failing, or being alone. Recall the early days and the freshness that Christ brought you.

Scripture Reading..

2 CORINTHIANS 5:17 NASB
Therefore if anyone is in Christ, he is a new creature; the old things passed away; behold, new things have come.

2 CORINTHIANS 5:21 NASB
He made Him who knew no sin to be sin on our behalf, so that we might become the righteousness of God in Him.

Reflection

How has your life changed since coming to faith in Christ? How are you presently growing?

I Want to Remember . . .

Today's takeaways from #LittleWomenBigGod are:

Day Four
My Favorite Scripture

When you hear people refer to their life verse, they are speaking about a Scripture that continues to encourage them over and over again. Sometimes we have verses that address different periods in our lives.

Scripture

List some of your favorite verses. Why are these special to you? What particular verse has God used to encourage you in your journey of faith?

Application

Organize the pieces of your story into a whole that will be easy for you to remember and tell. One of my friends uses photos of how she looked before she came to Christ. She was anorexic. Coming to know Christ literally saved her physical life as well as transformed her destiny. Choose a favorite Scripture to enforce your theme.

Practice saying it. Share it with friends and ask for feedback. If you are going through this study in a small group, take turns sharing your stories with other members of the group. The more you share your story, the more natural it will be to share when the opportunity arises. You may also want to put a written account in an album to leave for posterity.

Every story of faith is a miraculous part of God's story. I will share my story as an example.

My Story

Have you ever heard of bad luck changing a person for the better? In college, curiosity prompted me to join some friends on a weekend trip sponsored by a campus ministry. The dilapidated bus they'd secured for the trip was not up for the mountain climb to Gatlinburg, Tennessee, and repeatedly broke down. At each breakdown, various students took turns thanking God for our situation.

I believed in thanking God for good things, not for sitting in a freezing, stalled bus. Late in the night, hours after we should have arrived, another forced stop prompted me to add my silent prayer to the ones the other students offered. *Lord, don't listen to these people. They are crazy. Please get us to the retreat.* We made our destination in the wee hours of the morning.

During the weekend, a man shrugged off losing his senior ring. These students believed God reigned even in personal disappointments.

I knew Christ. In fact, I'd attended church since nine months before I was born. The message of God's love had touched me personally at a chapel service at church camp when I was in middle school. I remembered the brokenness and joy I experienced when I realized Jesus loved me enough to die for me.

But the exhilaration didn't last. Mama still told me to clean my room. My little sister continued to get into my stuff, and I still got irritated. I'd decided knowing Christ would take care of my eternity but had little to do with my daily life.

Being with these college students who trusted God with their disappointments awakened a hunger in me. I wanted to know God like they did.

I joined a Bible study that believed God's Word was living and relevant, not an antiquated story. I had always filtered out what seemed dated. When I applied the Bible's authority to my life, blindfolds dropped from my spiritual eyes. For the first time, the Bible made sense!

God used students who demonstrated faith in the middle of disappointment to show me God is at work in everything. I thank God for using a broken-down bus to open my eyes to the truth of Romans 8:28 (NASB). "And we know that God causes all things to work together for good to those who love God, to those who are called according to His purpose."

Your Story
Begin writing your story here.

_____

_____

_____

_____

_____

_____

_____

_____

_____

_____

I Want to Remember . . .

Today's takeaways from #LittleWomenBigGod are:

Your Story

Congratulations! Today you finish the study. I pray you will practice the lessons you have learned from the amazing women we've studied. And more importantly, may you continue to look to our big God, who is the same yesterday, today, and forever. Daily affirm his promises from Psalm 23.

- I believe my Shepherd provides everything I need, when I need it.
- I believe he is guiding my every step in the right way.

Scripture Reading...

ISAIAH 52:7
How beautiful on the mountains are the feet of those who bring good news, who proclaim peace, who bring good tidings, who proclaim salvation, who say to Zion, "Your God reigns!"

ROMANS 10:14–15
How, then, can they call on the one they have not believed in? And how can they believe in the one of whom they have not heard? And how can they hear without someone preaching to them? And how can anyone preach unless they are sent? As it is written: "How beautiful are the feet of those who bring good news!"

Application

Finish polishing your story. Read it aloud, and make any changes that are needed. Pray for opportunities to share it.

When you share your story, please, please do not speak poorly about any denomination. In fact, I think it's better not to name any particular church or Christian group negatively or positively. Of course, if you are talking to your church family about how your church has blessed you, then acknowledging their role in your growth is appropriate.

Otherwise, the particular group we're excited about may have hurt somebody in our audience. The branch of the church we're down on may be precious to them. Our emphasis should be to exalt Christ, not put up an obstacle for the listener.

Be creative and express your faith in a way that best reflects you. One of my friends helps women convey their personal stories of faith through scrapbooks and letters to their children, grandchildren, and loved ones. Your story will grow with your faith. Keeping a journal is one way to record God's faithfulness.

May God grant you great joy in your adventure of faith! And remember it is not the size of our problems, but the size of our God that determines the quality of our lives.

I Want to Remember . . .

Today's takeaways from #LittleWomenBigGod are:

Prayer Requests

Record your small group's prayer requests here.

Notes

Week One

[1]"Lexicon :: Strong's G4202 - *porneia*," Blue Letter Bible, accessed December 24, 2015, www.blueletterbible.org/lang/lexicon/lexicon.cfm?Strongs =G4202&t=NASB.

[2]"Lexicon :: Strong's G4203 - *porneuō*," Blue Letter Bible, accessed December 24, 2015, www.blueletterbible.org/lang/lexicon/lexicon.cfm?Strongs =G4203&t=NASB.

[3]Eric Metaxas, *Seven Men and the Secret of Their Greatness* (Nashville: Thomas Nelson, 2013), 149.

Week Two

[1]John F. MacArthur, *Hebrews,* MacArthur New Testament Commentary (Chicago: Moody Bible Institute, 1983), 364.

[2]"Lexicon :: Strong's G544 - *apeitheō*," Blue Letter Bible, accessed January 1, 2016, www.blueletterbible.org/lang/Lexicon/Lexicon.cfm?strongs=G544&t =NASB.

[3]Randy Alcorn, *If God Is Good: Faith in the Midst of Suffering and Evil,* (Colorado Springs: Multnomah Books, 2009), 4.

[4]Robertson McQuilkin, *An Introduction to Biblical Ethics*, 2nd ed. (Wheaton, IL: Tyndale House, 1995).

[5]Ibid., 439.

[6]Ibid., 441.

[7]Ibid.

[8]Ibid., 439.

[9]"Lexicon :: Strong's G5287 - *hypostasis*," Blue Letter Bible, accessed January 1, 2016, www.blueletterbible.org/lang/lexicon/lexicon.cfm?Strongs =G5287&t=NASB.

[10]"How Firm a Foundation," lyrics attributed to John Keith, published 1787, public domain.

Week Three

[1] "Ruth 4—Intermarriage," *ad Dei Gloriam* Ministries, http://addeigloriam.org/commentary/ot-history/ruth-intermarriage.htm.

[2] "2004 Indian Ocean earthquake and tsunami," *Wikipedia,* http://en.wikipedia.org/wiki/2004_Indian_Ocean_earthquake_and_tsunami.

Week Four

[1] Leviticus 25:23–27.

[2] J. Vernon McGee, *Thru the Bible with J. Vernon McGee,* vol. 2 (Nashville: Thomas Nelson, 1982), 106.

[3] Ibid., 107.

[4] "Lexicon :: Strong's H1350 - *ga'al,*" Blue Letter Bible, accessed January 5, 2016, www.blueletterbible.org/lang/lexicon/lexicon.cfm?Strongs=H1350&t=NASB.

[5] McGee, *Thru the Bible,* 142.

[6] Jessica Rey, "The Godly Truth about Bikinis," *godtube,* http://m.godtube.com/watch/?v=ooJF2MNU.

[7] Rey, "Godly Truth."

[8] Rebecca Adams, "This Is Why It's More Expensive to Be a Woman," *Huffington Post,* September 23, 2013, http://www.huffingtonpost.com/2013/09/23/beauty-products_n_3975209.html.

[9] "Lexicon :: Strong's H3671 - *kanaph,*" Blue Letter Bible, accessed January 5, 2016, www.blueletterbible.org/lang/Lexicon/Lexicon.cfm?strongs=H3671&t=NASB.

[10] Barbara Nicolosi, "Mom Was Right," *Church of the Masses,* May 11, 2014, http://churchofthemasses.blogspot.com/2014/05/mom-was-right.html.

[11] *Wikipedia,* s.v. "Levirate marriage," http://en.wikipedia.org/wiki/Levirate_marriage.

[12] *Dictionary.com,* s.v. "levirate law," http://dictionary.reference.com/browse/levirate+law.

[13] "Ruth 4—Biblical Genealogies," *ad Dei Gloriam* Ministries, http://addeigloriam.org/commentary/ot-history/ruth-genealogies.htm.

Week Five

[1] Amy Dickinson, "Teen victim looks for answers," Ask Amy, *Raleigh News and Observer,* February 26, 2013.

[2] "Lexicon :: Strong's H3947 - *laqach,*" Blue Letter Bible, accessed January 6, 2016, https://www.blueletterbible.org/lang/lexicon/lexicon.cfm?strongs=H3947.

[3] Kenneth Wuest, *Word Studies from the Greek New Testament,* vol. 1 (Grand Rapids: Wm. B. Eerdmans, 1973), 10.

[4] Cecil Murphey, *Making Sense When Life Doesn't* (Minneapolis: Summerside Press, 2012), 9.

Week Six

[1] Bill and Anabel Gillham, *Marriage Takes More Than Two* (Brentwood, TN: Wolgemuth & Hyatt, 1989), 8.

Week Seven

[1] A. C. Snow, "My Heart Takes Wing With Bluebirds," *Raleigh News and Observer*, June, 9, 2013.

[2] For more on how forgiveness, reconciliation, and trust relate, I recommend *Boundaries Face to Face* by Drs. Henry Cloud and John Townsend (Grand Rapids: Zondervan, 2003), 72.

[3] Matthieu Ricard, "The Habits of Happiness," TED, February 2004, https://www.ted.com/talks/matthieu_ricard_on_the_habits_of_happiness.

[4] C. S. Lewis, *The Problem of Pain* (New York: Harper Collins Paperback, 2001), 32.

[5] I heard Brennan Manning make this rhyme in the audio book version of *Abba's Child*.

[6] Charles Caldwell Ryrie, *The Ryrie Study Bible* (Chicago: Moody Bible Institute of Chicago, 1976, 1978), 983.

[7] Ibid.

Week Eight

[1] Kenneth Wuest, *Word Studies from the Greek New Testament*, vol. 2 (Grand Rapids, MI: Wm. B. Eerdmans, 1973), 46.

[2] "Lexicon :: Strong's G1135 - *gynē*," Blue Letter Bible, accessed January 7, 2016, https://www.blueletterbible.org/lang/lexicon/lexicon.cfm?Strongs=G1135&t=NASB.

[3] "Lexicon :: Strong's G435 - *anēr*," Blue Letter Bible, accessed January 7, 2016, https://www.blueletterbible.org/lang/lexicon/lexicon.cfm?Strongs=G435&t=NASB.

[4] Richard Exley, *The Indescribable Gift* (Green Forest, AR: New Leaf Press, 2002), 34.

Week Nine

[1] Macrobius, *Saturnalia* 2:4:2, quoted in Jimmy Akin, "Did the Slaughter of the Innocents Really Happen?" *National Catholic Register*, December 26, 2012, www.ncregister.com/blog/jimmy-akin/did-the-slaughter-of-the-innocents-really
-happen#ixzz2RKoC7Uu8.

[2]"Lexicon :: Strong's G4933 - *syntēreō*," Blue Letter Bible, accessed January 7, 2016, https://www.blueletterbible.org/lang/lexicon/lexicon.cfm?Strongs =G4933&t=NASB.

[3]Author's note: This should not be confused with roles that carry certain responsibilities. At the cross, Jesus provided for his mother's future. First Corinthians 7:32–35 and other Scriptures show that marriage and parenthood include the calling to provide for and attend to the needs of a spouse and growing children.